Strategic design

Eight essential practices every strategic designer must master

Giulia Calabretta,
Gerda Gemser &
Ingo Karpen

B/S

Colophon

BIS Publishers
Borneostraat 80-A
1094 CP Amsterdam
The Netherlands
T +31 (0)20 515 02 30
bis@bispublishers.com
www.bispublishers.com

ISBN 978 90 6369 445 6
3rd printing 2021

Copyright © 2016 Giulia Calabretta, Gerda Gemser, Ingo Karpen and BIS Publishers.
Copyedited by Jianne Whelton
Graphics by INK Strategy, layout by Dorus Galama

Content

Chapter 0 Introduction   6

Giulia Calabretta (Delft University of Technology), Gerda Gemser (RMIT University), Ingo Karpen (RMIT University)

0.1 The increasing importance of strategic design   7

0.2 What is strategic design?   9

0.3 Structure of the book   12

PART I – SETTING THE OBJECTIVES OF A STRATEGIC DESIGN PROJECT

Chapter 1 – Design Vision as Strategy: The KLM Crew Centre Case Study   20

Roald Hoope (Reframing Studio, Amsterdam), Paul Hekkert (Delft University of Technology)

1.1 Introduction   21

1.2 Vision creation – an overview   24

1.3 Vision creation – a closer look   29

1.4 Conclusion   37

Chapter 2 – Co-creating and Prototyping to Trigger Innovative Thinking and Doing   42

Giulia Calabretta (Delft University of Technology), Paul Gardien (Philips Design)

2.1 Introduction   43

2.2 Using visual and material artefacts for strategic purposes   46

2.3 Using co-creation for strategic purposes   51

2.4 Combining prototypes and co-creation: rapid co-creation at Philips Design   53

2.5 Conclusion   61

PART II – CONFIGURING A STRATEGIC DESIGN PROJECT

Chapter 3 – Designing Transitions: Pivoting Complex Innovation   68

Merijn Hillen (Fabrique), Jeroen van Erp (Fabrique), Giulia Calabretta (Delft University of Technology)

3.1 Introduction   69

3.2 Assessing the circumstances: shared vision and ownership   71

3.3 Four types of projects, four types of leadership   75

3.4 Conclusion   86

Chapter 4 – Creating Process Understanding: Design Practices and Abilities   92

Kasia Tabeau (Erasmus University Rotterdam), Gerda Gemser (RMIT University), Jos Oberdorf (npk design)

4.1 Introduction   93

4.2 Practices supporting process understanding   96

4.3 Abilities needed to support process understanding   102

4.4 Case studies   106

4.5 Conclusion   113

PART III – ORCHESTRATING A STRATEGIC DESIGN PROJECT

Chapter 5 – Aligning Organizations through Customer Stories   120
Marzia Aricò (Livework), Melvin Brand Flu (Livework)

5.1   Introduction   121
5.2   Principle #1: Nail the customer story   125
5.3   Principle #2: Translate the story across different business units   131
5.4   Principle #3: Design for multispeed impact   134
5.5   Conclusion   138

Chapter 6 – Designing for Feasibility   142
Gerda Gemser (RMIT University), Blair Kuys (Swinburne University), Opher Yom-Tov (Chief Design Officer ANZ Banking Group)

6.1   Introduction   143
6.2   A framework to assess feasibility   146
6.3   Case studies   150
6.4   Conclusion   161

PART IV – EMBEDDING A STRATEGIC DESIGN PROJECT

Chapter 7 – Making it Count: Linking Design and Viability   168
Nermin Azabagic (IBM Strategy), Ingo Karpen (RMIT University)

7.1   Introduction   169
7.2   Strategic design viability model   172

7.3   Step 1 – Setting up the business casing process   174
7.4   Step 2 – Developing and documenting assumptions   179
7.5   Step 3 – Co-creation of the business case, assumptions and solutions   181
7.6   Step 4 – Identifying key sensitivities for the implementation phase   186
7.7   Step 5 – Evaluate success of the design initiative   189
7.8   Conclusion   190

Chapter 8 – Lasting Design Impact Through Capacity Building   194
Ingo Karpen (RMIT University), Onno van der Veen (Ideate), Yoko Akama (RMIT University)

8.1   Introduction   195
8.2   Design principles   199
8.3   Leveraging and embedding the design principles in the client organization: Designers as coaches   204
8.4   Transformational design and cultural interventions   209
8.5   Conclusion   214

Chapter 9 – Conclusion   220
Giulia Calabretta (Delft University of Technology), Gerda Gemser (RMIT University), Ingo Karpen (RMIT University)

9.1   Strategic designers: Capital T-shaped professionals   221
9.2   Three-step approach for strategic design   223

GIULIA CALABRETTA
Delft University of Technology

GERDA GEMSER
RMIT University

INGO KARPEN
RMIT University

Introduction

0.1

The increasing importance of strategic design

The scope and influence of design is expanding rapidly these days. Organizations are increasingly adopting a design approach to define and implement their innovation strategies, using design to leverage organizational transformations, and even embracing design principles as the overarching philosophy that guides their entire organization. There are more and more Chief Design Officers (CDOs) leading innovation activities and fueling internal design culture – Apple's Jonathan Ive and PepsiCo's Mauro Porcini immediately spring to mind. Organizations like SAP and Microsoft are using design methods and practices to transform their product/feature-focused cultures into user-centered ones. And global business consultancies like McKinsey and Accenture have recently begun to acquire entire design agencies to better serve design-driven client needs. Even entrepreneurship is bonding with design, as start-up unicorns like Airbnb are not only being founded by designers, but make design principles the core of their offering and growth strategy.

As a consequence, design professionals are playing a more strategic role in the innovation. Designers are no longer mere executors of design briefs – they are involved in the crafting of the briefs, and guide the strategic decisions that underlie them. In order to effectively play this role, design professionals need to master a set of strategic practices – routinized ways of working – to address complex managerial challenges. When Mauro Porcini, CDO of PepsiCo, was tasked with establishing a design-driven innovation culture, he relied on prototyping processes and empathic thinking – two core design techniques – to deal with the conflicting interests of multiple stakeholders, the risk-adverse mindset of managers and the rigidity of organizational processes and structure (Ignatius, 2015). Porcini is a trailblazer in a newly emerging field of strategic design.

If you too want to learn how to act confidently and effectively within strategic design projects, this book is for you. This book proposes eight strategic design practices for design professionals who seek to grow or have already grown into a more strategic role in innovation. The practices are explained through tools and methods, and through case examples in which companies and designers have effectively used them. Additionally the book provides a set of guidelines that will enable design professionals to easily and quickly apply these practices in their next strategic design project.

Each chapter is dedicated to one strategic practice, and has been co-written by a combination of scholars and design practitioners. The design practitioners involved come from leading design agencies and renowned design-driven organizations both in Europe and elsewhere, while the academics are recognized scholars in the field of design and business, resulting in a book that provides design practitioners with actionable, state-of-the art knowledge on strategic design that is highly relevant for the field.

0.2

What is strategic design?

Strategic design refers to the professional field in which designers use their principles, tools and methods to influence strategic decision-making within an organization. Strategic decisions include those decisions that have a long term impact for companies, involve several stakeholders and require a substantial commitment of monetary and non-monetary resources. Examples of strategic decisions which strategic designers influence include the formulation of an innovation vision, and the identification of business opportunities related to the innovation vision. A designer's role becomes even more strategic if he or she is involved not only in the innovation strategy, but also in a broader range of strategic decisions like the company's overarching vision, corporate strategy and organizational culture. Indeed, design practices can become truly strategic if they are ingrained into an organization's culture and are allowed to drive most decisions, practices and behaviors within the organization. Companies like Apple or Airbnb are thriving examples of this highest degree of 'design strategic-ness' and proof that a strategic use of design can lead to superior performance and competitive advantage.

Do they want this?

Should we do this?

Can we do this?

Strategic design

Figure 0.1: Defining the domain of strategic design

The new generation of strategic designers needs to see themselves not as creative service providers, but as strategic partners in innovation decision-making. 'Strategic' implies being able to influence innovation decision-making by jointly and explicitly taking into account the *desirability, viability* and *feasibility* of the decision outcome – be that a vision, a business opportunity or a new product. For instance, if the task is to identify business opportunities in a new market, a CDO or a strategic design professional should help the company choose the opportunity based on a balanced consideration of the extent to which the opportunity fits the needs and wishes of people *(desirability)*, the assets and processes of the company *(feasibility)*, and the performance objectives of the company *(viability)* (Brown, 2009), as illustrated in Figure 0.1.

Desirability refers to the extent to which a project outcome meets the needs and wishes of people. People do not necessarily have to explicitly express these needs and wishes up front, as they can be 'latent'. For us, desirable implies that a strategic outcome should enhance people's lives. In other words, design is not simply about creating or fulfilling the wishes or needs of individual people – it is about enhancing their lives, and more broadly, creating a better society. Assessing desirability is one of a designer's fundamental prerogatives. Indeed, as the representative of the user/consumer perspective, designers are central to determining, influencing and assessing the desirability of any strategic outcome.

However, in line with reputed design agency IDEO, we argue that a strategic designer is one who not only decides on the basis of desirability, but also explicitly takes *feasibility* and *viability* into account. Feasibility means that the strategic project outcome can be given tangible or concrete form in the present, or in the foreseeable future, with the resources – technology, processes and people – available. Viability means that once the outcome is given a tangible form, that form can be sustained within the organization effectively enough to generate value in terms of relevant key performance indicators (KPIs) – profit, brand equity, triple bottom line, customer satisfaction – over the medium to long term. This strategic holism supports organizational acceptance of strategic design advice, and facilitates the actual implementation of the design initiative. Without implementation, there is no project, and your efforts will have been in vain. Thankfully, strategic design is co-creative in nature: a strategic designer does not make strategic decisions all alone – he or she needs a multidisciplinary team to co-create strategic decisions, including specialists in the domains that would impact feasibility and viability and other relevant stakeholders from inside the organization.

A strategic designer thus co-influences and co-decides on desirability, feasibility and viability. This is an iterative process, in which notions on what is desirable, feasible and viable may shift as part of the strategic design process; designers are warned not to blindly accept the organization's assessments of these factors at the project's inception. For example, while the vision developed by a strategic designer may not be immediately feasible because it cannot be implemented with an organization's current set of resources and capabilities, the organization may decide to 'stretch' their resource/capability set to actually make sure that the vision can be implemented. Or, while an organization may have set itself certain financial and commercial goals at the start of the project, and may wish to use these to assess viability, those goals may shift over time as more knowledge is gained during the design process as regards the problem and solution space.

0.3

Structure of the book

To be able to influence organizations' innovation strategy by balancing desirability, feasibility and viability, designers need to develop a different mindset, and acquire new knowledge, tools and methods to be up to the strategic tasks and decisions they are involved with. This book helps in this direction by providing eight valuable strategic design practices: envisioning, inspiring, simplifying, structuring, aligning, translating, embracing and educating. With the term practice we refer to an embedded or routinized way of working that is characterizing how designers work. These practices are organized in four parts, each representing a key stage or aspect of a strategic design project:

Part 1:
SETTING THE OBJECTIVES of a strategic design project

Part II:
CONFIGURING a strategic design project

Part III:
ORCHESTRATING a strategic design project

Part IV:
EMBEDDING a strategic design project

Part I, Part II and Part IV represent the sequential stages of a strategic design project, while Part III describes the ongoing, fundamental activity of a strategic designer. In each part, there are two chapters, each of which presents a different design practice. Every chapter contains a set of tools and methods that we believe will prepare designers to influence strategic decision making and balance desirability, feasibility and viability, and real-world cases that illustrate how the tools and methods can work in practice.

The choice to structure the book in four parts, with a related set of eight practices, is the result of our research on strategic design performed in the context of the four-year research project *Competitive Advantage Through Strategic Design*. The project was part of the Dutch Creative Industry Scientific Program (CRISP), which ended in 2015. CRISP focused on the design and management of product-service systems as a means to stimulate the continuing growth of the creative industry (www.crisprepository.nl). The program was partially funded by the Dutch Ministry of Education, Culture and Science, and by the Netherlands Organization for Scientific Research (NWO). In our research, we repeatedly observed and interviewed design professionals, design-oriented companies, and other stakeholders working with design professionals to better understand which design practices improve strategic (innovation) decision-making, and help companies achieve sustainable competitive advantage – and how they do so.

The first part of the book relates to *SETTING THE OBJECTIVES* of a strategic design project. This phase is about creating the right conditions for innovative thinking, and identifying the problem space that needs to be tackled. The two practices that support the effective execution of this stage are:

1. Envisioning
2. Inspiring

Envisioning relates to the practice of helping organizations incorporate a future-oriented, long-term perspective both into their innovation strategy and into the objectives of their strategic projects. In this chapter, design scholar Paul Hekkert (Delft University of Technology) and senior designer Roald Hoope (Reframing Studio, Amsterdam) describe how to discern future behaviors and use them to lend strategic direction to the activities of an organization. Their work builds on a reframing method co-created by Paul and a colleague, which Roald has applied in many different projects over the past 10 years.

Inspiring relates to the practice of making actors confident enough to think and act differently. This practice is elaborated on by academic Giulia Calabretta (Delft University of Technology) and Paul Gardien (Vice President of Philips Design). Their work looks at how designers can use visualization and materialization skills in a strategic manner, in order to persuade business stakeholders to embrace more innovative strategic directions and stay with them over time. They specifically focus on a rapid co-creation method as developed within Philips Design that is used to infuse digital innovation and service orientation into their offerings.

The second part of the book relates to *CONFIGURING* a strategic design project. This phase involves activities that help both to clarify the strategic problem space and prepare for the development of the solution space. The practices that belong to this phase are:

3. Simplifying
4. Structuring

Simplifying relates to the selection, connection and synthesis of information in a parsimonious and meaningful manner. This practice is elaborated on by creative strategist Merijn Hillen (Fabrique), Jeroen van Erp, co-founder of one of the largest design agencies in the Netherlands (Fabrique) and Professor of Concept Design (Delft University of Technology), and scholar Giulia Calabretta (Delft University of Technology). They present a framework to help designers determine which leadership style they should use, according to which circumstances, to effectively manage the complexity of a strategic design project. They support their instructions with real-world examples taken from Fabrique's portfolio.

Structuring refers to the practice of defining and executing each step on the road to achieving the project's objectives, while allowing for flexibility and sensitivity to changing circumstances.

This theme is discussed in a chapter written by scholars Kasia Tabeau (Erasmus University Rotterdam), Gerda Gemser (RMIT University, Melbourne) and Jos Oberdorf, who is a managing partner at Dutch design agency *npk design*, as well as a Professor of Product Architecture Design (Delft University of Technology). Based on an in-depth analysis of *npk design* working methods, the authors distil six practices and six abilities that help designers to foster a greater understanding of the creative design process in their clients. Creating process understanding, in turn, helps the strategic designer to successfully find and exploit opportunities within the organization.

The third part of the book relates to **ORCHESTRATING** a strategic design

project. The aim of this phase is to coordinate the different interests, objectives and expertise of the various stakeholders involved in the project. The related practices are:

5. Aligning
6. Translating

Aligning refers to steering the solution in a direction that complements or matches the organization's strategy, values and assets. This topic is examined by Melvin Brand Flu, director of strategy and business design at service design agency Livework, and Marzia Aricò, who is both a PhD fellow at Copenhagen Business School and a service designer at Livework. They describe how aligning requires a profound understanding of both how customers behave and how a business works. Key insights from their practice underscore three main principles: construct a well-formulated customer story, translate the story across different business units and design for multispeed impact.

Translating refers to the practice of converting information from one language to another – verbal to visual, visual to verbal, tacit to explicit, explicit to tacit – to enable knowledge sharing and knowledge creation. This topic is examined by two scholars, Blair Kuys (Swinburne University, Melbourne) and Gerda Gemser (RMIT University, Melbourne), and designer Opher Yom-Tov, who is currently Chief Design Officer at ANZ Banking Group.

They recommend that designers explicitly take feasibility into account during the design process, as this will enhance the chances of actual implementation. They point to the need to perform an 'audit' of an organization's resources and capabilities to assess feasibility, and provide guidance as to how this should be carried out.

The fourth part of the book relates to EMBEDDING a strategic design project. The aim of this phase is to ensure that the outcomes of strategic design projects are implemented, and strategic design advice adopted on a more permanent basis. The related practices are:

7.   Embracing
8.   Educating

Embracing relates to the practice of creating widespread organizational commitment to the project outcome, and to the design approach used during the project. The chapter is written by Nermin Azabagic (IBM Strategy) and scholar Ingo Karpen (RMIT University, Melbourne), and focuses on viability. The authors describe viability management throughout the design process, using the well-known Double Diamond model to structure how aspects related to viability play a role. They also describe how assessing viability is an iterative process to be co-determined by designers and other specialists in the design team.
Educating relates to building design

capacity among organizations by teaching them the ins and outs of design. This chapter is written by scholars Ingo Karpen (RMIT University, Melbourne) and Yoko Akama (RMIT University), and Onno van Veen, partner at service design agency Ideate. The authors show how six design principles that characterize design can also be used to frame designers' efforts to educate organizational stakeholders. The chapter shows how designers can help organizations adopt and internalize these principles through coaching and cultural interventions, and in doing so build design capacity within those organizations.

In our epilogue, we three co-authors envision a future where design is a core strategic capability within every organization, and list the characteristics of strategic designers who help weave design into the fabric of an organization's strategy and innovation process.

References

Brown, T. (2009). Change by design,
HarperCollins (New York)

Ignatius, A. (2015). "How Indra Nooyi
Turned Design Thinking Into Strategy",
Harvard Business Review, Sept: 81–85.

PART I

Setting the objectives of a strategic design project

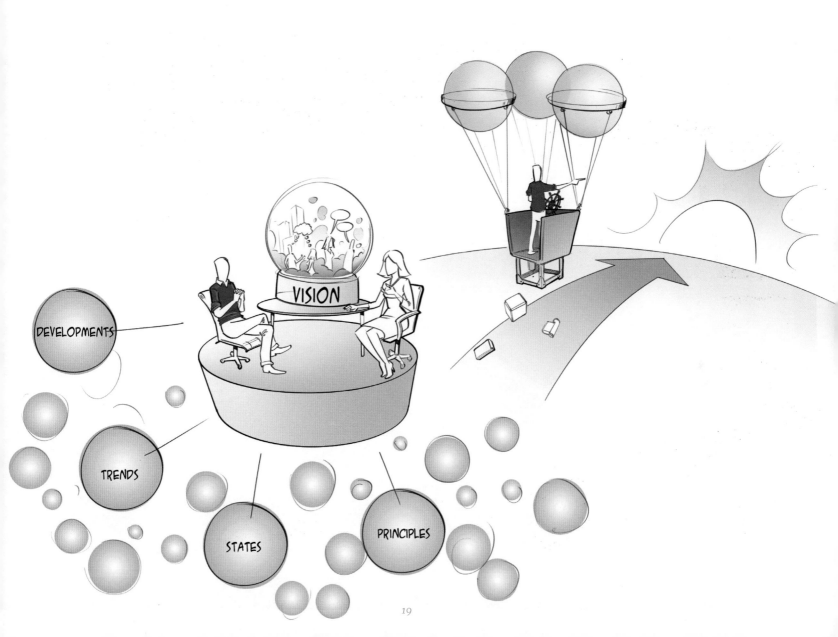

01

ROALD HOOPE
Reframing Studio

PAUL HEKKERT
Delft University of Technology

Design Vision as Strategy:
The KLM Crew Centre Case Study

1.1

Introduction

What if strategy and innovation professionals could peer into the future? Not in a way where they would see everyday reality, but in a way where they could sense how the underlying fabric of that reality shapes the needs, wants, desires and behavior of future generations? Would this vision of a possible future help these professionals to expand their horizons and explore new opportunities? Would it help them understand where they need to be in the future and make plans for how to get there? Would it not give them an edge over their competitors? Of course it would, but seeing the future is clearly impossible. Or is it?

Forecasting and market-oriented vision development has been the subject of research for decades (e.g., Schwartz, 1996; van der Heijden, 2005). This research demonstrates that by using people-centred methods (e.g., Brown, 2009; Dorst, 2015) to structure and facilitate a vision of a possible future, designers are – to a reasonable extent – able to predict where society is heading. These future perspectives are not crystal clear, but opaque – their possibilities naturally depend on human behavior. While they may not be entirely 100% accurate, they are predictive enough to make a huge difference for organizations that want to prepare for what is to come. One of these future vision creation methods is Vision in Product Design or ViP (Hekkert and van Dijk, 2011), and one strategic design firm that is specialized in working with this method is the Dutch agency Reframing Studio.

Reframing Studio positions itself as a design and innovation consultancy who specializes in using a design approach to broaden the strategic thinking and workflow of client organizations, and enables them to generate various outputs – products, policies, visions – for long-term success and societal impact.

The first author is a senior designer and consumer insight specialist at the studio where he has worked for more than ten years now. He has applied ViP, which they call Reframing, with different types of clients, including large multinationals, SMEs, service companies and non-profit organizations. For all these projects, Roald and his team at Reframing Studio started by developing an in-depth understanding of human behavioral patterns, beliefs, values, habits, desires, motives, emotions and needs, and translated this into a possible future, with a set of related product/service opportunities. With this kind of project, their intention is not to simply solve the problems of the present, but rather to explore future opportunities, and provide a vision that lends a strategic direction to the activities of their clients.

Over the course of several weeks, the second author, Professor of Industrial Design at Delft University of Technology and co-inventor of the ViP method, interviewed Roald several times at the studio about how he works with organizations to create visions of the future. His methodology is appealing for design professionals and innovation strategists to learn from and try for themselves. The first part of the interview will give design professionals a broad idea of the approach, and illustrates how the approach was applied in one of Reframing Studio's most recent projects for Dutch airline KLM. The second part provides a closer look at the way Roald and the team at Reframing Studio create possible visions of the future. We will conclude this chapter by briefly looking at ViP from the client perspective.

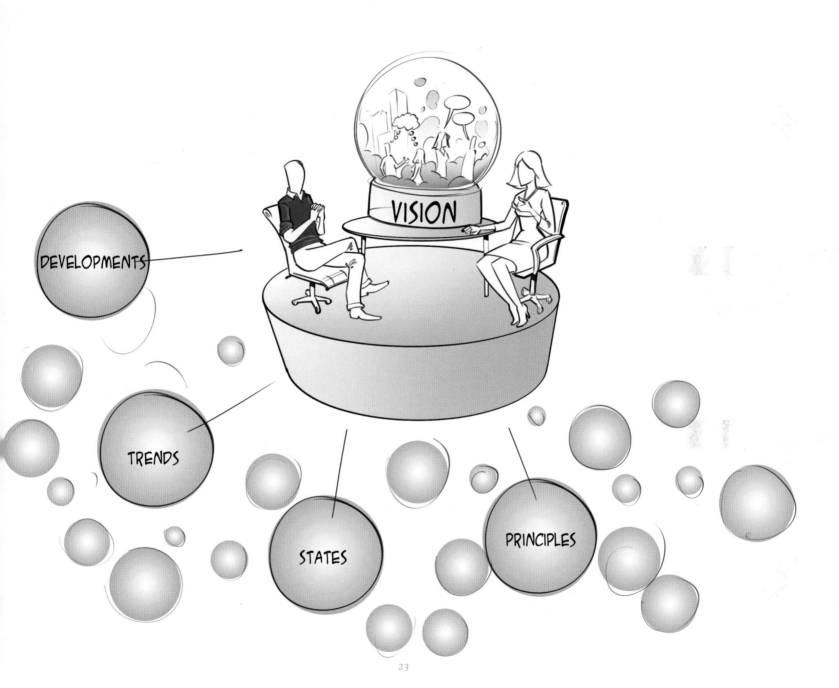

1.2

Vision creation – an overview

The core of the ViP or Reframing methodology is the act of developing a future vision that both directs the designers' activities, and can shape a design concept that will be meaningful for people in the future.

ViP starts by mapping the world of tomorrow in a specific, pre-defined domain – the *context*. Several building blocks – *context factors* – can be classified into two main categories:

- Factors that point to *changing patterns*, referred to as *developments* or *trends*. For example, 'people are eating out more and more these days'. Developments and trends indicate which human behaviours have changed or are changing, and these changes can be quite meaningful to an organization and its future activities.
- Factors that capture *stable patterns*, called *states* or *principles*.

For example, 'people are inclined to reciprocate gift giving'. *States* and *principles* prevent designers from narrowly focusing on changes in the world, which might hinder their ability to perceive the patterns underlying them – stable forces of nature, common human behaviors, and cultural norms and customs.

By consulting publications, scouring the Internet and delving into a variety of secondary sources, designers can identify the building blocks or ingredients of the possible future context. One very valuable resource is the wisdom that can be provided by experts. These might be employees of the client organization, or external parties with expertise in the domain in question. Experts are not expected to solve problems or generate ideas. They are brought in to help the designer gain a deeper perspective of the matter, and reveal the factor patterns that impact the domain.

After dozens – or hundreds – of these context factors have been generated, then begins the complicated task of making sense of the data. All these states and principles, all these trends and developments must be brought together into a coherent, unified view of the domain under review. This vision, which typically takes the form of a framework, is the key deliverable of any ViP process, and it gives a strong direction to any subsequent design or strategy the designer creates.

Before we dive into the process of vision creation, I'm curious to know how you would define the word 'vision'?

'For us, a vision is an educated prediction of people's future attitudes and behaviors in a specific area of life, and the motives and concerns that fuel those behaviors. A more thorough understanding of how people will behave in the future, and why, helps give design professionals and their clients a better grasp of the "hidden forces" that will shape our future world, and hence the products, services and policies that will resonate with people in the future.'

'The vision anticipates a variety of specific behaviors that are likely to exist in the future. A vision reveals multiple possible behaviours in a certain area of life. These behaviours can be exhibited simultaneously by different people, and sometimes consecutively by a single person.'

'As the KLM case will demonstrate, these possible future behaviors don't necessarily come across as novel – some are not exactly "futuristic". Often we reveal latent or undetected potential behaviors that might have been present all along. And these persistent behaviors can be the most relevant to the future context.'

So how do you go about creating a vision? Where do you start?

'We start by defining a domain, and delimiting its scope. The domain is the research topic, the subject that requires a new vision. Domain titles should be formulated to express the perspective of users, consumers or citizens, rather than the perspective of the organization. It could be an area of life, or a daily task like 'cooking' or 'urban mobility'. The scope is the time frame – how far will the vision look ahead? This is usually somewhere between 5 and 20 years.'

Some companies aren't used to looking five years – or more – into the future. How do you get their management to look beyond the status quo?

'Choosing a domain and determining its scope can be challenging for an organization that has come forward with an urgent problem that they want the designer to address. I usually tell them that we will deal with the urgent problem later, and solve it much more effectively, if we first gain a more accurate picture of the domain in which this problem exists. Interestingly enough, it often happens that the focus will shift away from the urgent problem altogether, simply because the client gets carried away with the possible opportunities that lie ahead. Of course we love it when that happens.'

Once you have defined the domain and scope, what's the next step?

'When the domain and scope have been defined, the designer then begins interviewing key stakeholders, and domain experts. Stakeholders are the decision makers and influential people inside the organization – including the people that designers may need to have on board in case the vision changes course later on. Interviewing them and involving them in the process will not only provide designers with pertinent insights, but that connection will reinforce organizational commitment to the outcomes. It is important for designers to understand the organization's perspective, and be sensitive to its needs and concerns. The goal is not to please the client *per se*, but rather to know when events are – or are not – proceeding in line with organizational expectations, and be consciously prepared to account for any actions that may deviate from these.'

'Besides interviewing stakeholders, designers need to decide if more input is needed. It happens that stakeholders also have the relevant expertise to reliably identify a domain's developments and trends, and other factors like cultural norms and customs. Other times, an external expert can be brought in to provide insight into the factors that have proven to influence behavior in the domain.'

What kind of questions do you ask them to start out with?

'The best way to get to the factors is indirectly, by starting the conversation and continuing the questioning in directions that both parties find interesting. Usually, an interviewee will at some point explain what needs to be done – what they see as the "solution" to a problem in the domain. I then try to find out how they came up with this solution. On which objective observations was this solution based? The goal is to be meticulous about separating "observations" from "opinions", to arrive at a value-free outlook on the domain. Opinions become important at a later stage, when discussing how the organization wants to affect this outlook.'

How do you know when to stop collecting input?

'Initially, the idea is to try to get a balanced mix of factor types – an even number of developments, trends, principles and states that shows diversity in the fields they pertain to. The final outcome is a wide range of cultural, sociological, psychological and technological factors that remain within the scope of the domain. When factors become redundant, that is a good indication that every avenue has been explored. We also ask the experts if they think the list is complete.'

You mentioned that this might lead to a list containing hundreds of factors. Is that workable?

'No, hundreds of factors are by no means workable. They need to be clustered based on the qualities and meanings they share, rather than by topic. The general direction emerges from bringing such disparate factors together. There can be up to 20 clusters, with some containing only one or two factors. The goal is to have as few clusters as possible without losing the

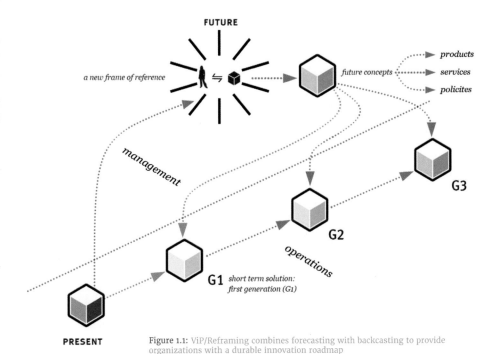

FUTURE

a new frame of reference

future concepts

products
services
policites

management

G3

G2

operations

G1 *short term solution:*
first generation (G1)

PRESENT

Figure 1.1: ViP/Reframing combines forecasting with backcasting to provide
organizations with a durable innovation roadmap

richness of the individual factors. The clusters are presented as a kind of trend analysis report, and they are called the 'driving forces' of the domain. However, unlike the macro-trends in a trend report, the clusters are specific to the domain, and they consist partly of stable factors like cultural norms and customs, some of which are obvious but highly relevant nevertheless.'

Is that the vision?

'No, it's an intermediate step. Designers cannot really construct a possible future domain until they make sense of the relationships between the clusters, those driving forces. Do the clusters support each other, or do they compete? Are there abstract similarities between them? Designers should strive to distill the complexity of the future domain into a visualization – a model or framework of some kind that resembles the simple formulas scientists use to explain complex processes. We typically arrive at a two-dimensional axis model, or a four-field matrix. But a Venn diagram or pyramid might also be suitable. These visual frameworks portray the interplay of the diversity among possible behaviors that ultimately reflects the needs, desires and concerns that may emerge in the future of a specific domain. The framework is the embodiment of the vision, the *framework is the vision.*'

So you have a framework that reveals possible future behavior in a specific domain. Then what do you do with it? How do you put it to use?

'The designer and organization up to this point have strived to remain objective. Now the organization is asked to take a stand in relation to the possible future of their domain. Sometimes an organization does not agree with an emergent behavior. In that case they can choose to actively counter it with new future products and services. More often, the organization wants to know the extent to which they have already addressed some of the behaviors, and if there are uncharted areas to explore. The organization can plot their current product and service portfolio against the framework to see how well their offering addresses the full spectrum of future concerns, information that can be used to direct the development of new products and services in areas where they are currently not active. So at Reframing Studio, we actually *combine* forecasting and backcasting. First we look ahead, and make an educated prediction about people's future attitudes and behaviors in a specific area of life, then we work our way back and identify products, services or policy programs that will connect the future to the present (see Figure 1.1).'

'There are times when it is too difficult for an organization to empathize with the behavior and the underlying concerns, as these may appear to be too "new", too subtle or too improbable. When that's the case, it helps to develop a number of exaggerated and rather bold concepts that perfectly address the future behaviors while ignoring the limitations that exist in the world of today. These ideal embodiments of the vision help organizations to understand where the vision is steering them. They are like little dots on the horizon. It is important to generate a very small number of these future concepts, because otherwise organizations will begin to perceive them as actual design outcomes, whereas you want them to be seen as examples of future opportunities that lie in a certain direction.'

'Once the organization has identified their stance as regards the vision, we help them develop ideas for the short and medium term, and usually help them place these on an innovation roadmap.'

1.3

Vision creation, a closer look

At the crew centre at Schiphol Airport (see Figure 1.2), KLM crew members prepare for their journeys. On a recent trip back from China with KLM, the second author asked several crew members to describe their individual pre-flight preparations – how they prepare their uniforms, the protocols they observe, their contact with new colleagues and the silent routines that make up their daily duties. Flight crews do not know always personally their colleagues, but they know exactly how they will act in any given situation.

Efficient crew centre layout and organization play a vital part in this preparation stage, and KLM commissioned Reframing Studio to rethink its process and facilities. In the recent past, a student design project had provided KLM with some 100 ideas to improve the current situation. Yet what KLM actually needed was a frame of reference, a coherent vision that would enable them to choose the idea with the most promise. They then turned to Reframing Studio.

Figure 1.2: A section of the KLM crew centre at Schiphol before the project started

Describe the KLM crew centre.

'It spans three floors of an office building at KLM's hub, Schiphol Airport. The airline employs roughly twelve thousand flying personnel, including flight attendants and pilots. These people do not work regular hours. A lot of them work part-time, and work a flight once every one or two weeks. Staff rarely work with the same colleagues. New crews are formed for every flight, so it's not often that you see your colleagues more than once in your career. The crew centre is the closest thing to an office that they have. And the familiar faces of the people that work there are one of the few stable factors in their working life.'

Why do they form new crews for every flight?

'KLM sees this as the most efficient way to run a very complex organization. Manning tens of thousands of flights each year is a logistical feat of gargantuan proportions. Keeping crews together would only make things more complex. But flying with a regular crew also has its benefits. Once "tuned into" each other, the crew could reach an optimal performance level. However, familiarity can tend to blur the boundaries between professional roles, and some behavioral patterns are formed which can serve as a disadvantage to overall team performance.'

'Crew performance is influenced by a complex interplay of factors. For example, passenger satisfaction survey results show that passengers are slightly less satisfied with the crew on return flights.

Can this dissatisfaction be attributed to the "role blurring" as described above, or to the different mix of passengers on homebound flights, or can it be explained by the fact that nighttime departures occur more often at airports other than the hub? We know that crew performance has a significant effect on passenger satisfaction, so that is all the more reason to study the interplay of these elements in-depth.'

What happens at the crew centre, exactly?

'A lot of practical things take place. Crew members need to check in, and then they usually drop off their hold luggage. Because crew members get a daily allowance for each layover day, there are also ATM machines they visit to withdraw cash in various currencies.'

'Staff members are on hand to solve urgent problems on the spot – from expired passports to troubles at home. Crew members can check the roster, and request changes. Each of the twelve thousand employees has their own personal post box, used to spread internal memos and other corporate communications. Some employees are actually quite attached to their own little pigeon hole.'

'There are two main user groups, each of which observes a slightly different set of pre-flight routines. The cabin crew, consisting of flight attendants and pursers, goes to one of the briefing rooms for a flight briefing. This is the first time that the people who are going to fly together will have met. Over the course of twenty minutes, the cabin crew learns about passengers with special needs and new safety procedures – anything out of the ordinary really. After the pre-flight briefing, the crew jointly exit the crew station and head for the gate.'

'The cockpit crew, consisting of pilots and co-pilots, has their own space to prepare for the flight. Together, they calculate how much fuel to load, check the latest weather reports, and plot the safest route. They have usually finished their preparation once the cabin crew arrives.'

'These are largely procedural issues. But there is also a lot of socializing and waiting going on. Check-in time is ninety minutes before the flight, but lateness cannot be tolerated, so the crew usually leave quite a margin to be safe. They arrive early, and have extra time to spend. They have coffee, make small talk or talk to their loved ones on the phone before heading out.'

Do you remember what KLM asked you? What was the briefing you got from them?

'When we got involved, KLM had already started a project aimed at improving the crew centre. They were determined to involve the users – the crew – from the very start. This meant organizing several co-creation sessions. The marketing and branding department also had several ideas for improvements, as did the company responsible for facilities management. So at one point there were literally a hundred ideas that had come from multiple directions. Around that time, the project became known as the "Moodstreet project". We got involved some time after that.'

"Moodstreet"? That sounds interesting.

'Let me briefly explain what it means. Imagine you are a flight attendant getting ready for work, a process that takes several steps. You may start your day in jogging pants, looking all scruffy. But at some point you freshen up, do your hair, shave or put on some make-up. After that, you pack, get dressed and head out the door. At Schiphol you begin to feel the buzz of the airport. There is more and more KLM blue around you. You meet your colleagues and start to get a feel for what's going on in the air, what's in store for this particular flight. Remember that KLM is a full-service carrier – you are expected to be your best self when interacting with passengers. This means getting into the right mood. Comparable to going through a car wash, called a "wash-street" in Dutch – so, "mood-street", there you have it.'

In the end, what was the brief that Reframing Studio got?

'Well the team was struggling with decision-making. They were in need of arguments that would impact their choosing one decision over another.'

'For big projects with massive numbers of stakeholders, sound arguments keep everyone on board. They wanted to be able to demonstrate the value of the "mood-street" to everyone involved.

developments

When a factor concerns a phenomenon that is currently changing, or one that is expected to change in the near future, it is called a development.

trends

A special class of developments is constituted by factors concerning tendencies in the behaviour, values, or preferences of (groups of) people. Such developments we often specify as trends.

states

A state is a surrounding world condition that will probably not change in the near future, but does not have to be necessarily fixed. States are (or appear to be) relatively stable at the moment of observation.

principes

Principles are factors that are, by their unvarying nature, constant over longer (and longer) periods of time. The term refers to immutable laws or general patterns that can be found in human beings or nature.

Figure 1.3: Examples of four different types of context factors, all obtained from interviews with experts at KLM

Including higher management. This is exactly why we typically use Reframing – to ensure that we have a clear and future-proof notion of the reasons that prompted the design. And we then use it to make sure that the reason – the "why" – is aligned with the "how" and the "what"'.

'KLM needed a new frame of reference for their ideas – a vision that could help

them determine an idea's relevance, and discern the "good" ideas from the "bad" ones. They were also open to the possibility that their idea generation may not have been exhaustive, despite the huge number of ideas they already had. So the project team asked us to help them develop a framework they could use to move forward.'

KLM crewmembers are very good at quickly forming tightly nit teams. They have no prior experience with one another and must perform their task almost immediately upon formation. In research literature these teams are called Swift Starting Action Teams (STATs) and 'swift trust' plays a crucial role in the proper functioning of these teams. Swift trust is forwarded trust; a high level of trust is assumed initially, despite the premature nature of the relationship. Only later the level of trust is verified and adjusted if needed.

Swift trust occurs when team members are aligned 'a priori'. Explicitly through clearly defined roles and responsibilities of individual team members, and implicitly through a rich company culture, strong group norms and habits and similar backgrounds in education. This shared language forms a solid basis for cooperation. Swift trust needs to occur in just the right amount. Too much of it can cause complacency and a lack of mutual monitoring. Too little can lead to conflict.

Figure 1.4: Example of a cluster of ten factors which describes a phenomenon that influences human behavior in the domain of 'crew performance in 2019'

How did KLM's needs translate to the ViP/ Reframing methodology?

'KLM asked us to develop a future vision of the domain of "crew performance" with a five year scope. They wanted us to tell them what the crew centre would mean to the crew. So we needed to look at the domain from the perspective of a crew member – a typical brief. We start out with a domain and a scope and get to work.'

Do you formulate a domain and scope together with the client?

'Yes, we do – especially the scope. We suggested looking far into the future, because a few of the current issues had bogged them down.'

'Consider, for example, those 12,000 post boxes, and the spatial and practical logistics involved in maintaining them. Although crew members had an almost fanatical attachment to them, the existence of present-day technological advancements makes them virtually unnecessary. Everyone agreed that in five years, internal communications would be completely digitized. So once we had agreed on that future outcome, the work became a matter of designing a smooth transition. A temporary opt-out system was designed that would make the boxes compulsory, and later, an opt-in system would enable crew members to turn theirs in voluntarily. Once the domain and scope have been defined, it becomes much easier to work backwards.'

After defining the domain and scope, whom did you interview?

'Well first of all, we needed to know what the crew centre was like, how it fit into a working day.'

'Next, we spoke to experts from different branches of KLM. We asked if they had noticed changes in crew behavior over the years, how they would describe the corporate culture, what technological developments they saw coming and how these could affect crew performance. Another common question was, "How do you see the crew centre in the future?"

'Interviewees will describe an aspect, and it is the designers' job to find out *why* they feel this is important, which can reveal factors that had not been considered previously. For example, one interviewee told us that in the future there wouldn't be a crew centre anymore – crew members would check-in online, get all the info they need, and meet each other at the gate. The first part about the crew centre becoming obsolete is a personal opinion, which could be true, but it's too early to tell. The second part describes all kinds of technological developments, which could influence the domain profoundly. These we are interested in.'

Can you give me some more examples of factors you deemed relevant to this domain?

'People judge an experience largely based on how they felt at its most intense point, the peak, and at its end. This "peak–end rule" is a *psychological principle* coined by Daniel Kahneman, I believe (Kahneman, 2011). We didn't know it then, but this ended up being a very relevant factor found in the literature.'

'Another example is the increasing vulnerability of the crew's public image, a *cultural development*. Not many professions require employees to continually face hundreds of people, all of whom are invisibly connected to hundreds of other friends and contacts. Crew members are always in the spotlight, so any missteps could easily damage the brand.'

'These are just two examples. From the interviews and literature we collected over a hundred factors. The final outcome was seven clusters comprising roughly 15 factors each.' (See Figures 1.3 and 1.4 for more examples.)

What did the vision look like? What kind of model did you create for KLM?

'Our model enabled the project team to step into the shoes of the crew for the entire work cycle of a single flight, including the time leading up to departure and the time after the journey had ended. The model offers a vision of the domain of crew performance in 2019. It describes fifteen states of mind that influence the behavior of a crewmember during the course of an entire working day. Some of

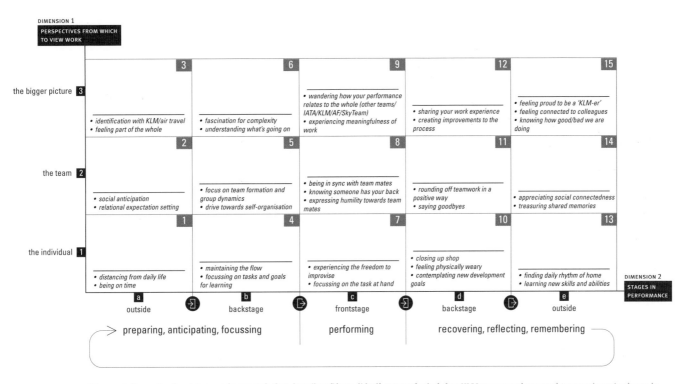

DIMENSION 1
PERSPECTIVES FROM WHICH TO VIEW WORK

the bigger picture 3

3

• identification with KLM/air travel
• feeling part of the whole

6

• fascination for complexity
• understanding what's going on

9

• wandering how your performance relates to the whole (other teams/ IATA/KLM/AF/SkyTeam)
• experiencing meaningfulness of work

12

• sharing your work experience
• creating improvements to the process

15

• feeling proud to be a 'KLM-er'
• feeling connected to colleagues
• knowing how good/bad we are doing

the team 2

2

• social anticipation
• relational expectation setting

5

• focus on team formation and group dynamics
• drive towards self-organisation

8

• being in sync with team mates
• knowing someone has your back
• expressing humility towards team mates

11

• rounding off teamwork in a positive way
• saying goodbyes

14

• appreciating social connectedness
• treasuring shared memories

the individual 1

1

• distancing from daily life
• being on time

4

• maintaining the flow
• focussing on tasks and goals for learning

7

• experiencing the freedom to improvise
• focussing on the task at hand

10

• closing up shop
• feeling physically weary
• contemplating new development goals

13

• finding daily rhythm of home
• learning new skills and abilities

DIMENSION 2
STAGES IN PERFORMANCE

a — outside
b — backstage
c — frontstage
d — backstage
e — outside

preparing, anticipating, focussing   performing   recovering, reflecting, remembering

Figure 1.5: Example of a vision – a framework that describes fifteen 'ideal' states of mind that KLM crew members need to experience/embrace in order to perform at an optimal level. The first, second and fourth columns were found to be most relevant for the crew centre

these states of mind were familiar. We also revealed latent or undetected states of mind that had been present for some time. These states of mind – novel or familiar – would drive the most relevant behavior in the future context.

'We found that crew performance has two main dimensions. One reflects the psychological aspect related to upholding performance standards. Similar to actors, the crew begins to prepare for the coming performance mentally, privately, at home. Backstage, on-site, the crew members don their costumes, and get into character – the setting and the proximity of the performance time create a sense of excitement and anticipation. Then the performance begins, after which there is time to recover and reflect again, backstage. This theater metaphor was borrowed from one of my favorite sociologists, the late Erving Goffman.'

'The other dimension relates to the

shifting perspectives of crew members as regards their work and their profession. On an inward level there are personal concerns for punctuality, enthusiasm and professionalism. Outwardly, there is the awareness of being part of a team, and beyond this lies the crew member's sense of connection with the KLM brand and the wider aviation industry. Because crew members increasingly operate autonomously, it is important for them to see how their actions relate to a global, ceaseless logistical mechanism.'

'The fifteen states of mind are a result of the interplay between these two dimensions. Five performance stages, multiplied by three perspectives for looking at the job, gives a total of fifteen states of mind (see Figure 1.5). These states of mind underlie all future crew behavior, and shape the future world. Products and services that address these states of mind will resonate with the crew and will likely be successful.'

Did the project team understand the model right away?

'Most were personally familiar with the work cycle, so it was easy for them to empathize with the states of mind, even the emergent ones. A lot of states of mind pass by in this single work-cycle. The project team was actually quick to recognize where KLM was doing well and where they were under-performing.'

How did the project team apply the vision framework?

'They recognized that the better all states of mind were addressed, the happier crewmembers would be and the better he or she would perform. This would lead to greater passenger satisfaction and, subsequently, a higher repurchase intention, the holy grail of airline performance indicators. The model showed us where KLM needed to put their energy to help the crew reach optimum performance levels.'

'The project team then asked us to help them select the best ideas from the pool that they had already gathered. We selected the ideas that fit the framework, and plotted them on it.'

'For example, one idea put forward suggested that an "inspiration tree" be placed near the entrance to the centre, so that crew members could leave inspirational messages for one another. The framework calls for that area to be dedicated to the transition from "outside" to "backstage", so any communicative content should deal with the KLM brand, social media feeds and passenger satisfaction feedback, ideally displayed in digital format. We shifted many ideas through the framework to where they would fit, or eliminated them. Then we developed ideas for the areas that were neglected. For example, the existing ideas were entirely oriented toward the outbound crew – the crew leaving Schiphol. There was basically no functionality for the incoming crew. But we knew the inbound crew often felt out of place, like they were "in the way". So we included ideas to address this part of the framework.'

'From this selection of ideas, we then developed a coherent concept. A lot of good ideas bundled together still don't make a good solution – it was important for Reframing Studio to make sense of them, and orchestrate the final experience, so that the users experience the overarching idea.'

1.4

Conclusion

This chapter started out with an overview of the ViP/Reframing method. We then illustrated how the approach was used to create a vision for the future in a recent project for KLM, the Dutch airline. We will conclude by briefly looking at ViP/Reframing from the perspective of the client.

We interviewed Els Polhuijs who, in her role as Vice President of Cabin Inflight Management, was responsible for products and services on board. She was the project owner of the KLM Crew Centre project, and as such was ultimately accountable for the success or failure of the project.

Can you recall to what extent the method was useful for KLM at the time?

'The framework had great practical value for us. We thought we completely understood the crew and their concerns, and we found out that we were close, but that there were still a few areas in need of attention, like the important role the return flight plays in overall crew performance, or crew preoccupations with thoughts of home when getting ready for work. The framework actually formed the basis for our new internal flying personnel communications strategy. We used it to attune the flow and tone of our communication to their varying states of mind.'

Besides these broader strategic implications, how did it help in moving the crew centre project ahead?

'Of course, the crew centre plays a role in our communication with the crew as an important means of communication. But we are always looking for smart ways to cut costs, and were prepared to ask ourselves tough questions, like "do we really need a large crew centre?" The vision Reframing Studio developed helped us answer this question in exactly the right way. Yes, we do need a crew centre, but it can be just as effective using a much smaller footprint. We need the centre to foster a healthy bond with our personnel, almost like a clubhouse where they can reliably touch base. The states of mind showed us what the crew could need at any stage in their working day, and we used this insight to determine the minimum requirements to effectively address these needs. It turned out we could do with approximately half the floor

flight safety and product
integrated information stand
subjects: flight safety, in-flight products
tools: display case, screen and poster frame

dynamic food bar with host(ess)
food & juice bar serving
fresh sandwiches and salads
quality serviced coffee

self service coffee machine
self service espresso machine
social high tables
high tables facilitating an open and dynamic
interaction between employees and crews

brand area
'window display of the brand'
with brand objects on display:
new trolley, consumer objects, etc.

inspirational displays
clusters of hanging screens
products displayed in tables

lighted backdrop
hanging circles defining the area
and stimulate feeling of belonging
by providing shelter

floor
different floor to define
the area and stimulate
feeling of belonging

self service food
fast lane option
quality food vending m
microwave for heating

Figure 1.6: Visualization of the new design of the KLM crew centre

area. This provided us with considerable impetus to move the project forward – a well thought out plan we could implement for less' (see Figure 1.6 for the new design of the KLM crew centre).

'The process is deceptively simple –

collect factors and postpone judgment; neatly weave these into a pattern that yields a particularly compelling perspective (the vision), and then decide on a course of action. Yet building a coherent vision that will drive organizations forward requires more

skill than it might appear. Designers are trained to connect factors, building blocks and emergent behaviors with the designed world. One of a designer's core skills is an ability to see the connections between contextual factors and possible design.'

About the authors

ROALD HOOPE is a senior designer and consumer insight specialist at Reframing Studio in Amsterdam. Roald is responsible for developing forecasts of future consumer behaviour and translating these insights into opportunities for new products, services and policies. Roald holds a master's degree (cum laude) in Integrated Product Design from Delft University of Technology, Faculty of Industrial Design. He started his 15-year professional career as a designer at Norit (now Pentair), where he was responsible for creating a line of water purification products for the international consumer market. He gravitated toward the front end of the new product development process, and started at Reframing Studio in 2004 where he built a track record fusing consumer insight development with design. Recent clients include Ahold, Aegon, KLM, NS, Google and Philips. At Delft University of Technology, Faculty of Industrial Design Engineering, Roald coaches bachelor design students learning to apply the Reframing/Vision in product design (ViP) innovation method in the course 'Design Driven Innovation'. He also shares his expertise with business professionals as a trainer at Reframing Academy, Reframing Studio's own training institute.

PAUL HEKKERT is full professor of form theory and head of the Design Aesthetics group at the Faculty of Industrial Design Engineering, Delft University of Technology. Paul conducts research on the ways products impact human experience and behavior. He has published articles dealing with product experience and aesthetics in major international journals, and is co-editor of *Design and Emotion: The experience of everyday things* (2004) and *Product experience* (2008). In 2011, he received a VICI grant from the Dutch Science foundation (NWO) to develop a Unified Model of Aesthetics (UMA). Together with Matthijs van Dijk, he published *Vision in Design: A guidebook for innovators* (2011), a book that describes an approach to design and innovation that has been widely applied in both education and industry. Paul serves as a member of the editorial boards of *The Design Journal*, *Empirical Studies of the Arts*, and *International Journal of Design*. Paul is co-founder and chairman of the Design and Emotion Society and former chairman of the executive board of CRISP, a national collaborative research initiative for and with the Dutch creative industries. He is also member of the Dutch Creative Council, and scientific member of the Top Sector Creative Industries.

References

Brown, T. (2009). *Change by design: How design thinking transforms organizations and inspires innovation. New York: HarperCollins Publishers.*

Dorst, K. (2015). Frame innovation. Cambridge, MA: MIT Press.

Goffman, E. (1959). The presentation of self in everyday life. New York; Anchor Books.

Hekkert, P. and van Dijk, M.B. (2011). *Vision in design: A guidebook for innovators. Amsterdam: BIS Publishers.*

Kahneman, D. (2011). Thinking, fast and slow. New York: Farrar, Straus and Giroux.

Schwartz, P. (1996). The art of the long view. New York: Doubleday.

Van der Heijden, K. (2005). Scenarios. The art of strategic conversation. Chichester: John Wiley.

02

GIULIA CALABRETTA
Delft University of Technology

PAUL GARDIEN
Philips Design

Co-creating and Prototyping to Trigger Innovative Thinking and Doing

2.1

Introduction

Embracing new business opportunities, changing an innovation strategy and pursuing radically new innovations are performance enhancers for any organization. Yet such measures are threatening, as they often introduce uncertainty and require risk-taking behaviours.

Managers and their organizations often resist these choices, thus stifling innovation in their companies. Managers think about themselves as rational decision makers, and like to follow courses of action whose outcomes they can predict and assess. This is not always possible with innovation, where intuition and leaps of faith are important triggers. Similarly, most organizations run smoothly thanks to stable infrastructures and consolidated processes – the 'performance engine' – which further facilitates a solid return on investment. Yet, however dependable they are, these ingrained processes act as deterrents to embracing the cutting-edge business innovations that would likely subvert them.

Through their mindsets, attitudes and modes of working, strategic designers have proven themselves capable of disrupting companies' routines and inspiring managers to think and act differently. By introducing design thinking into the company culture, and by encouraging employees to experience user research and human-centered design, the Chief Design Officer of the software company SAP managed to shift the innovation focus – in both strategy and mindset – from 'functional excellence' to 'superior user experience'. By using design methods, Dutch airline KLM is empowering innovative initiatives at every level of the organization, and is transitioning its mission into becoming the most customer-experience focused carrier in the market.

There are two aspects of designers' way of working that are central to the objective of inspiring companies to think and act differently – designers' frequent and purposeful use of visualization/materialization techniques, and their adoption of co-creative approaches that incorporate an end-user perspective throughout the design, development and implementation of a strategic project (Calabretta and Gemser, 2015). In this chapter, we will illustrate how and why these two elements can break down resistance to change and innovation, and show how electronics, healthcare and lighting giant Philips has reaped the benefits of combining these two core practices in their 'Rapid Co-Creation' approach to innovation.

2.2

Using visual and material artefacts for strategic purposes

Naturally, design professionals frequently use material and visual artefacts during any project they are involved in. Visualizations and materializations include all the ways designers structure and present information – not as text or numbers, but as images, maps, objects and stories.

In strategic projects, materializations and visualizations are tools that help designers translate opportunities into tangible and observable manifestations. The 'realness' of these – and of the experiences they inspire in stakeholders – can reduce uncertainty, and encourage the organization to open up to more innovative possibilities. It is often difficult for designers to explain how the emergent future might look to an organization whose culture is conservative, or set in its ways – but when presented with something they can interact with, organizations are given the opportunity to conceive of that future for themselves, and to reflect more creatively and concretely on the potential of a given innovation strategy.

Visualization tools like *customer journey maps*, *storyboards*, *personas* and *prototypes* help designers and innovation teams to inspire stakeholders' emotional engagement with a designed innovation, targeted end users or even a new technology. These tools also create a shared language between disciplines, and allow designers to deliver huge amounts of complex information in forms that neatly instruct, inform and engage their audiences. All too often, clunky market research reports end up in cabinets, or on forgotten thumb drives. Visualizations make data memorable, and actionable. For example, customer journey maps and personas – two ways to efficiently summarize research results – facilitate internalization of the information organizations need to assess and pursue truly novel changes. Infographics, animations, posters and digital visualizations condense complex information – market intelligence, technical processes/expertise, company vision, innovation strategy – into comprehensive and clear images that serve as a call to action. The surge in the number of design agencies specialising in producing visuals – think XPLANE, JAM and INK – attests to their power.

Within this trend of using visual thinking as an inspiration to strategic action, materialization in the form of prototypes plays an important role, especially in the early stages of strategic planning, when stakeholders are required to lower their resistance to and generate commitment for innovative courses of action. *Early prototyping* permits the testing of different ideas and concepts in a rapid and iterative fashion. Through early prototyping, design professionals provide tangible artefacts that allow stakeholders to experience vivid manifestations of the future, and develop commitment to new directions. A very important characteristic is that (early) prototypes are incomplete by definition, and thus invite stakeholders to exchange and develop their own ideas, build on the ideas of others and ultimately develop a sense of collective ownership of results. For instance, designers working with a printing solution provider used early prototypes to explore market applications and related business opportunities for a new kind of elevated printing technology – a printing technology that can print multiple layers of ink to a height of 5mm. By involving key stakeholders – business developers, marketing managers, R&D managers – in the process of prototyping potential applications for the architecture and interior design industry, designers persuaded business stakeholders of the potential and versatility of the technology. Thanks to their 'hands-on', iterative development process, the early prototypes increased business stakeholders' sense of ownership and commitment, which were essential to their introduction into an industry they had never dealt with before. Prototypes are not only for product materialization – they often illustrate the use of novel services and elaborated experiences. Stakeholders 'undergo' an experience to better evaluate its impact. This experience can also be produced through 'low fidelity' methods, like role-playing.

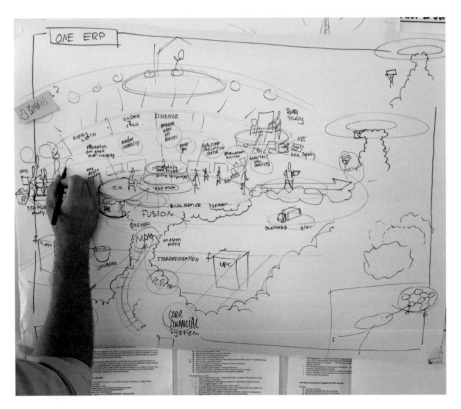

Visualizations, prototypes and their related practices are highly effective ways to develop strategic projects and call organizations to action. That effectiveness can be maximised if the designer keeps the following four features in mind:

1. *Keep it simple.* Strategic visualizations are intended to make an uncertain future more approachable. Thus, any new technologies, early prototypes and potential new market scenarios should be presented using simple representations that depict essential information. Designers should not aim to showcase their drawing skills, but rather to spark the imaginations of relevant stakeholders.

2. *Leave it incomplete.* If the aim is to solicit feedback and inspire action, undeveloped or incomplete visuals might – surprisingly – be what is required (see Figure 2.1). For instance, presenting a customer

journey map that has only been sketched out, which stakeholders are invited to complete with their own first-hand observations of user behaviours, will better serve a strategic purpose than a full-scale customer journey where designers have filled in all the blanks – including new business directions. Also, detailed visualizations trigger detailed questions that are not yet relevant in the early stages of a project. On the other hand, conceptual visualizations trigger general observations about the overall idea. Moreover, if the visualization is too detailed, some stakeholders may assume that the general idea has already been fixed, and fail to see how their contributions matter.

3. *Plan the making process.* The process of creating a visual or material artefact together with a stakeholder

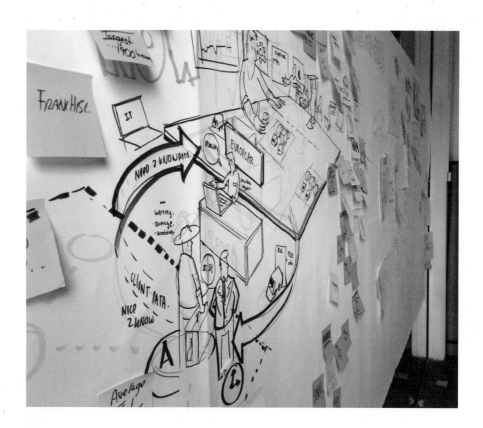

Figure 2.2: An intermediate step in the making of INK visuals

might be more valuable than the artefact itself. That is why strategic designers should not only choose strategically which visualizations/ materializations to use, but also plan carefully which steps should be followed – and thus demonstrated or taught – in their execution, and whom should be involved. For instance, strategic visual design agency INK helps companies visualize their strategies through a series of design workshops where the collaborative process of asking questions and finding answers jointly leads participants to a deeper internalization of the strategy (see Figure 2.2).

4. *Combine languages.* Many business stakeholders see themselves as rational decision makers. They are used to relying on analytical processes, and prefer to use quantitative data to drive action. While visual and material artefacts utilising images and stories might inspire managers to think differently, combining that visual language with numbers and facts can help designers achieve the desirable dual result of inspiring stakeholders to both think and act differently – and to make decisions that are grounded in reality. That is why personas that include market data like segment size, growth and market share, or tools like the 'business model canvas' – which combines visuals of value propositions with cost/ revenue estimations – are preferred by design professionals who wish to influence strategic decision making. (Please refer to Chapter 7 for more on this topic.)

2.3

Using co-creation for strategic purposes

Design professionals also use the practice of *co-creation* to both inspire stakeholders' willingness to explore business opportunities, and maintain their commitment to such opportunities over time. Strategic design professionals must stimulate stakeholders' active participation in every stage of opportunity development, and so plan frequent interactions with them – participation and co-creation encourage stakeholders to consciously devote cognitive effort to innovation activities, unconventional ideas and design-driven methods. As many of the chapters in this book will demonstrate, inviting stakeholders to take an active part in the project develops ownership of the strategic design process and of its innovative outcome, which ultimately reduces the perceived risk of innovation, and increases the chances that the project will make it to the implementation stage.

An additional bonus to co-creation is that it may promote ongoing collaboration. Successful co-creative processes establish connections and reciprocal trust that can be used to nurture further collaboration between designers and the organization or among stakeholders – from implementation of the business opportunity to the development of a product/service portfolio or the application of a method to a different context. Because designers tend to scout for a broader array of stakeholders to be involved in co-creative innovation activities, this ultimately may result in more widespread engagement with co-creation as a day-to-day practice within the organization. This is especially important. The problems that we face today as a society are incredibly, and increasingly, complex – consider the aging of our populations or the rising cost of our healthcare systems. These problems require systemic changes at a number of levels, and learning how to co-create solutions is a must – not only to generate solutions, but also to achieve consensus for those solutions.

To ensure that co-creation is effectively used for strategic purposes, designers should keep the following advice in mind:

1. *Recruit broadly*. Strategic projects have broad impact within a company – they affect the concerns and interests of a variety of stakeholders

while requiring their support. To be better able to change an organization's course of action, designers should cast their nets wide in search of the broadest array of internal and external stakeholders possible. Through co-creation, synergies are created between stakeholders who do not typically cross paths. These are precisely the kinds of connections that produce new knowledge and ideas that have never been considered before.

2. *Structure co-creation activities.* Clear outcomes and deliverables are important metrics – and boundaries – for organizations. Thus, designers should define deliverables and eventual performance outcomes for each co-creation session upfront, moderate the sessions such that those deliverables are achieved and use what has been defined co-creatively to inform the subsequent stages in the innovation process. Getting stakeholders involved in creative sessions where sticky notes are hung on crowded walls does inspire, but participants will be better able to leverage that

inspiration if they can see how their creative efforts will be funnelled into actionable and potentially measurable outcomes. Typically, around halfway through a co-creation session, participants start to doubt if anything useful will come out. A well-structured process will help participants to move through that uncertainty – a process that prepares them for the uncertainty inherent in any innovation process. With co-creation, design professionals regularly help strategic innovation stakeholders to trust the process.

3. *Keep control of the process.* Co-creation seeks to catalyse a variety of different expertise. To maximize the odds of project success and the maintenance of its innovativeness, responsibility for key decision-making moments should be clearly assigned to the most competent individual/stakeholders. For instance, when using co-creation to explore alternatives, and select and pursue new opportunities, co-creation sessions could be used to identify possible directions and

assemble a broad range of relevant perspectives. The results of the session should then be used by the project owner as guidelines to aid in the selection of the best direction – based on the information provided, and other feasibility and viability considerations (please refer to Chapters 6 and 7 for more on these topics). Thus, designers should learn to balance co-creative moments with independent decision-making, and to assign responsibility for independent decision-making to the most appropriate stakeholder for the task.

4. *Plan for multiple iteration loops.* Designers should try and get user feedback on possible solutions as soon as possible, and as often as possible. For instance, one approach could be to plan a one-day or two-day co-creation session, and then plan a longer, one-week session to ensure that the team both obtains insight as rapidly as possible, and does not waste time pursuing directions that do not resonate with end users. Only too often, people fall in love with their own ideas and stick with them far too long.

2.4

Combining prototypes and co-creation: Rapid Co-Creation at Philips Design

Royal Philips of the Netherlands is a technology company focused on improving people's lives through meaningful innovation. Royal Philips has a broad portfolio in the areas of healthcare, consumer lifestyle and lighting, and it has recently begun focusing more on the healthtech area. Philips' in-company practices show how co-creation and visual/material artefact creation can be effectively combined and used to inspire cultural change and alter stakeholder behaviour (Gardien, Rincker, M., and Deckers, 2016). Like a number of other companies, Philips is now embracing the paradigm shift from the industrial and experience economy to the knowledge economy, where innovation occurs at an ecosystemic level, and where different stakeholders contribute and become intertwined in delivering meaningful experiences to customers. More and more people are seeking evolutionary experiences, capable of changing and growing with them, that are uniquely their own. These are delivered through constantly expanding ecosystems of offerings – interactions between products, services, portals, apps and digital content – that entail multiple transactions. An example of

such an evolving ecosystem is Philips Hue. Starting from internet-enabled light bulbs that can be controlled via an app to create personalized atmospheres, Hue has evolved into a complete ecosystem involving third party apps, connection to other devices such as televisions, additional lighting and switches, interactive story books, and so on. Innovating in such a context is different, as the linear 'waterfall' innovation process followed before cannot enable parties to grasp the interconnectedness of the ecosystem that incorporates all the relevant players harmoniously. Philips – like many other companies – has had to adapt to this novel way of innovating, and has found in co-creation a useful way to inspire business stakeholders to embrace the mindset and organizational changes required for them to commit to the innovation. Philips Design – the design department within Philips, from now on referred to as 'Design' – has played a strategic role in facilitating such transformation, especially by helping different stakeholders understand the needed changes by framing visual and material narratives of the ecosystem that will immediately make sense to end users, to other departments in the company and eventually to other players in the ecosystem. Design methods, the fostering of a designerly mindset and employing designerly modes of work have emerged as particularly suitable ways to ignite and consolidate change, given their ability to reduce perceived risks and make unconventional and unexpected futures approachable and even engaging. Design has created a framework, dubbed 'Co-creating Innovation', and developed a method within it, which we call the 'Rapid Co-Creation approach', to help Philips move forward. The Co-creating Innovation framework focuses on creating meaningful propositions for business opportunities in the ecosystem and, through an iterative process, enabling the company to improve and implement those propositions. The Rapid Co-Creation (RCC) approach aims at accelerating acceptance and implementation by translating the proposition into a prototype and iterating on it (Calabretta and Perez, 2014). The Co-creating Innovation framework is visualized in Figure 2.3.

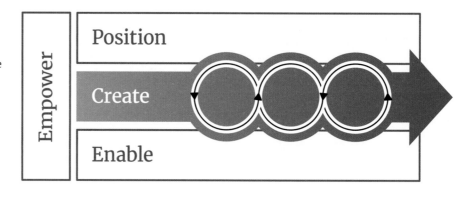

Figure 2.3: Philips' Co-creating innovation framework

The framework starts with a *position* stage, where different stakeholders identify relevant business opportunities and derive meaningful propositions to iterate on. Research findings from different sources and different methods, together with knowledge of current products and services and understanding of company resources, assets and capabilities drive the positioning stage and the creation of the proposition. Propositions are then regarded as hypotheses to be tested through RCC (the *create* stage), as only through experimentation and fast iterations can Philips really understand whether a proposition is truly relevant to people, technically feasible and viable for their business. In order to be carried out effectively, RCC needs to be supported by an infrastructure that enables the realization of the prototype, and any technical iterations it has (the *enable* stage). Such infrastructure includes, for instance, IT systems, hardware and software components and even privacy policies. Given the iterative and non-linear nature of co-creation, the three stages run simultaneously. In parallel to them, the *empower* aspect creates support within the company for design-driven co-creation, and design thinking in general, by conducting training courses on RCC that are open to everyone – especially to people who do not belong to the Design community. This activity is fundamental to increasing the odds of a 'soft landing' for the innovative propositions and prototypes that may come out of the RCC approach.

Within the Co-creation Innovation framework, RCC is one of Philips' core methods (see Figure 2.4). RCC best exemplifies the inspiring power of combining prototypes – strategic visualizations – with a co-creative approach. Different internal and external stakeholders are involved throughout the process, generating enthusiasm and commitment for the innovation outcome and its implementation. The RCC approach is not novel – it is based

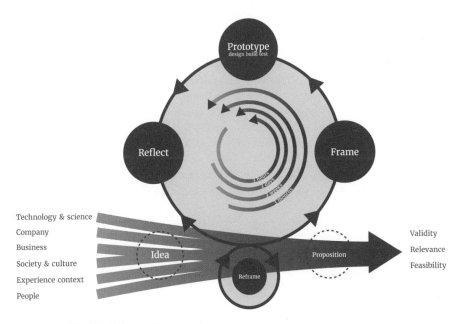

Figure 2.4: Philips' Rapid Co-Creation approach

on design thinking as developed by a number of eminent design companies and professionals, but for a large company with a manufacturing tradition it can be regarded as radical. Thus, Philips – and Design – is exemplar in the way it has

renovated and upgraded these approaches in order to make them work within the Philips context.

Design started RCC in 2009, initially with the aim of establishing a structured approach for internal Philips start-ups. As the method includes rapid testing of the minimum viability of a proposition – called 'experience demonstrators' in Philips' language – and creates momentum around innovative ideas, RCC was subsequently formalized and used to win acceptance for innovation in different contexts. As Philips aims more and more at becoming a digital company, RCC is now commonly used to develop digital innovations that enrich Philips' product offer. The agile and collaborative nature of RCC makes it the ideal approach to pursue digital innovation – which needs to be fast, close to users, well integrated with physical products and continuously evolving. Furthermore, compressed versions of it are used to create innovation awareness and openness with C-suites within the company, and within partner organizations in our ecosystems.

RCC is based on quickly developing testable hypotheses for a value proposition (*Frame*), embedding them into basic prototypes and testing them as quick as possible (*Prototype*) in order to elevate the value proposition to the next step (*Reflect* and eventually *Reframe*). The iteration loops can have different lengths – hours, days, weeks, months – depending on the application area. For instance, if RCC is used for training purposes or to sensitise C-suites, then a 3-hour dip in the pool is sufficient. When the RCC is used to develop (digital) products, then going through as many loops of different lengths as possible is actually the most effective approach. RCC is the approach Philips has followed to develop digital innovations like the Smart Air Purifier, an app that allows users to track and control the air quality in their living quarters, through its connection with an air purifier device; The HomeCooker Next, an app-controlled cooking device; and the GrandBaristo Avanti coffee maker, a high-end espresso machine that allows coffee control and customization via a tablet.

In the following paragraphs, the main elements of the method will be discussed in some detail and by means of examples.

Preparation
One of the key learnings from Philips experience with RCC is that preparation is key to really keeping the process fast, effective and grounded in the bigger picture of Philips and the relevant ecosystem. For each RCC process, the project leader and selected team members, representing different areas of expertise, schedule several preparatory meetings to discuss the technological and market domain (including the target segment), define key roles and responsibilities and set a tight but feasible timetable. With everyone on the same page beforehand, proposition framing and prototyping can start from day one. During the domain discussion, the team is extended to include top management, as the embedding of the RCC initiative can only occur if its outcome fits the growth strategy of the company.

Defining and assigning roles and responsibilities for the entire process is also an important part of the preparation. During the initial stages and the first rapid loops, designers play a central and leading role, as their coordination is fundamental. Leading the sprints and keeping a diverse team of specialists working harmoniously together is a difficult task that designers can execute very well, as collaboration is part of their DNA. Especially during the sprints, designers move ceaselessly from one expert team to another – from IT experts to business modellers, to UX designers, for example – to align the prototypes, keep the focus on the common goal, facilitate interactions and motivate everyone to remain committed to (radical) innovations.

Framing (and Reframing)
Once the team is set up and the context is well understood, RCC can begin by formulating a clear and specific proposition for iteration and eventual reframing. Especially at the beginning of RCC, propositions are very hypothetical and everyone should be aware and open to the fact that the chance of distortion is high. To build relevant, clear and testable propositions, the multi-disciplinary team can use a 'framing canvas' (see Figure 2.5), which relies on the research conducted in the preparation stage, and helps the team to reflect on the critical elements that need to be balanced in order to develop a strong proposition – business viability, technological feasibility, relevance to people and society and the desired user experience. By answering the facilitating questions suggested by the framing canvas, different insights are combined in a proposition that expresses Philips' actual

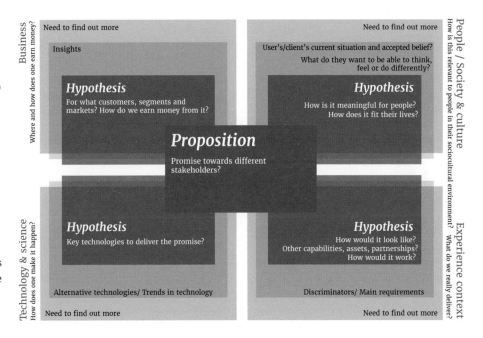

Figure 2.5: Philips' framing canvas

promise to the different stakeholders

Prototyping
Once a proposition has been framed, the multifunctional team enter a phase of rapid and repeated prototyping and testing. Within RCC, the prototyping process aims to deliver experience

prototypes whose aim is not so much to explore and perfect a technology, but rather to articulate the desired user experience by confronting users with an artefact as soon as possible, even if this implies 'faking' some parts of the solution. These quick-fire iterations are made possible – and rendered effective

– through parallel prototyping. For the smart Air Purifier, sub-teams with different expertise worked in parallel and iteratively on prototyping artefacts in three relevant domains – the *user*, with running versions of the customer journey map, personas, experience flow and user interfaces for the digital products; the *business*, with prototypes of the business model canvas, the revenue model and the stakeholder/ecosystem map; and the *technology*, with product prototypes showing the potential technological architecture, hardware, connectivity and data platform. All prototypes are kept 'quick and dirty' to elicit feedback at the end of any sprint day, when the project leader leads an alignment discussion of the desirability, feasibility and viability of the day's outcomes.

At the end of each loop, the prototype is tested with users. This can also be regarded as a co-creative effort, since very often the qualitative methods for user research preferred by designers – ethnography, observations, in-depth interviews – are combined with more quantitative market analytics and survey results obtained by market intelligence analysts. This combination of methods not only seeks to provide thorough and quantifiable support for the market potential of the evolving prototype, it also seeks to follow a rational/analytical approach to decision-making regarding the prototype's upgrade.

As previously noted, the iterative loops can have different lengths, from several days – three days minimum – to several weeks or several months – three months maximum. The 3-5 day sprints, usually referred to as *hackathons*, are a distinctive element of the approach, as during these sprints motivated teams of design professionals, business/marketing people, engineers, developers and innovation experts lock themselves in inspiring spaces to workshop and translate cutting-edge (digital) opportunities into user, business and technology hypotheses to be validated with a lead user. During these sprints, there is no right or wrong way to go, since the aim is to learn as much as possible from experts and users in preparation for the next iteration. In the case of GrandBaristo Avanti, the RCC team hunkered down in the Saeco headquarters in Italy, just a flight of steps away from the factory floor, as previous experience had shown that being close to production facilities accelerates the prototyping process and especially prevents avoidable feasibility errors. In a mere few days, the GrandBaristo team combined different work modes, expertise and personal interests to effectively inject digital transformation and a service mindset into a traditional manufacturing business. The result was a proposition for a coffee machine where each coffee could be tailor-made to suit the tastes of the users by means of a tablet.

The proposition is then submitted to relevant stakeholders for additional iterations, further features specification and ultimately full-scale development. Since keeping the pace is key, iterations and RCC team meetings remain frequent after the *hackathons* are wrapped up.

Reflection
During the RCC process, time is set aside to reflect on what has been accomplished so far and determine how to go on. This reflection involves all the aspects of the proposition and of the prototyping process. Knowledge of user desirability and experience, business viability and technological validity should all reach the same level of maturity. Moreover, reflection is a true team effort – it is crucial that all participants, stakeholders and roles fully engage in an open and honest dialogue. Open-mindedness is crucial – each team member should be ready and willing to see unexpected opportunities and challenges, and be open to change their personal hypothesis. During every hackathon, at the end of every day, every sub-team presents its daily achievements, informally tests the achievements of the other sub-teams and defines joint objectives for the following day.

All in all, RCC benefits strategic design projects in many ways, especially in terms of the collaboration between strategic designers and business stakeholders. Working side by side on different prototypes offers everyone the opportunity to familiarise themselves with and develop trust in each other's expertise, working modes and priorities. In particular, the experimental setting of the RCC approach helps business stakeholders to gradually embrace innovative ideas that they might have regarded as risky and not viable at the beginning. For instance, in the case of the GrandBistro Avanti, the RCC approach led managers to embrace the idea of changing their revenue model from selling high-end espresso machines to selling a product/service system – a high-end espresso machine combined with a digital customization service. Thanks to the limited scale and investment required by RCC, the hands-on working style, the feedback from frequent user tests and team empathy, different stakeholders were able to experience first hand the strengths and pitfalls of digital and service innovation, act upon them and ultimately gain some control over the unknown – in this case, ownership of the GrandBistro Avanti.

Obviously the transition from an RCC outcome prototype to the market still presents some challenges. While RCC delivers an MVP – minimum viable product – through an agile, rapid process, the momentum might get lost once the prototype is handed over to a development team that may operate using a more standard, linear process, and might follow a more analytic decision-making process. One of the solutions is to ensure that resources move *with* the proposition into the next phase, especially a long-term project leader who can work across teams, and over time.

2.5

Conclusion

From Philips' experience in implementing the RCC approach over recent years, a number of lessons can be drawn from both the method itself, and the more general benefit of combining visual/material artefacts and co-creation techniques in order to inspire innovation and organizational change.

1. *Business involvement and commitment are crucial.* RCC cycles can deliver great prototypes and business opportunities that show enormous potential. However, all this potential gets lost if there is no commitment to following up on these opportunities. Thus, RCC or any other co-creation approach should not start without the involvement and the tangible commitment – capacity and budget – of business owners. (Please refer to Chapter 3 for more on this.) Furthermore, it is the designers' responsibility to translate co-creation outcomes – especially if they are radical – into a roadmap that will facilitate their adoption and implementation by the company.

2. *Strategic designers should play a neutral, 'facilitator' role.* As co-creative processes involve several stakeholders across cycles of intertwined activities, the facilitator plays a key role. This role is even more important for RCC, where co-creation occurs in a compressed time frame. Strategic designers can play this role particularly well, as they are trained in collaborative work as 'T-shaped professionals' (see the Conclusion for more on this) with core expertise in design, and essential levels of knowledge in all other innovation-relevant disciplines – including engineering, marketing, technology, and so on. As facilitator, the strategic designer helps the co-creation team to *become* a team, *act* as a team and *constructively reflect* on their own actions and lessons learned. The facilitator ensures that the team does not miss opportunities, and does not get stuck in a certain

direction. However, it is difficult to combine the neutrality that effective facilitation requires with designers' own expertise in desirability. As it is important that the 'people perspective' is well represented, the designer-facilitator might show a degree of bias – or be seen as biased – their commitment to represent the users may unconsciously steer the team towards solutions that might overemphasize desirability at the expense of feasibility and viability. For co-creation and RCC to be successful, different designers with different roles should be present – some should lead and facilitate co-creation, some others should focus on desirability of the solutions, and perhaps some others could take care of the visualizing processes, activities and outcomes.

3. *Research should be conducted throughout the process as a parallel activity.* One of the risks of RCC is that the emphasis on speed might make the innovation efforts too shallow. To prevent that,

research should accompany the entire process, and cover different aspects. Early stages (*preparation* and *frame*) should be focused on understanding the company and how the outcome of RCC will fit within the existing product portfolio, brand, capabilities and assets. Furthermore, user research on the lifestyle domains for which RCC will develop solutions is also important. For instance, if the aim of RCC is to develop a proposition for monitoring and improving individual lifestyle habits, then gaining in-depth scientific and user knowledge on topics like sleep and lifestyle change improves the team's prototyping and reflecting capabilities. The level of research depth and specificity increases all along the process, and may even lead to involving specific knowledge experts in the co-creation team.

4. *Designers should be able to assess the required prototyping fidelity levels.* The ideal level of 'visualization' to present to users and stakeholders is

the subject of ongoing debate. There needs to be a balance between what is needed to get the right feedback at a particular stage in the process, and a level of clarity and completeness that both inspires stakeholders and makes them confident in taking decisions.

As we, as a society, move towards more systemic and volatile problems and solutions, the ability to visualize preferable future directions and to develop them quickly, iteratively and with a firm end-user focus to ensure that people will recognize and adopt the solutions is of utmost importance. Design and design thinking have a key role to play in developing these solutions, but in order to deliver on this promise we need to embed them well in every organization. The proper use of visualization techniques and co-creation methods plays a key role in developing sustainable solutions that have the confidence of many stakeholders and meet the challenges of today and tomorrow.

About the authors

GIULIA CALABRETTA is Associate Professor in Strategic Value of Design at the Faculty of Industrial Design Engineering, Delft University of Technology. Giulia has a marketing background, as she got her Master's Degree in Management and Marketing at Bocconi University (Italy). She also holds a PhD in Management Science from ESADE Business School (Spain) and a Post Doc from BI Norwegian School of Management (Norway).

Giulia believes that design and design practices are the right way to go for making companies more innovative in their DNA and preparing them for the behavioral, technological and cultural revolutions of the future. So her current research focus is on understanding how design practices and capabilities can be effectively and permanently integrated in the innovation strategy and processes of companies. Additionally, she is interested in what makes a great Chief Design Officer and why each company (and institution) should have one.

Her research has been published in such journals as *Organization Studies*, *Journal of Product Innovation Management*, *Journal of Business Ethics*, *Journal of Service Theory and Practice*, *Journal of Service Management*.

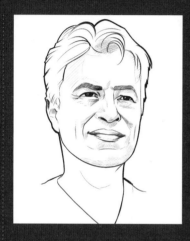

PAUL GARDIEN is Vice President of Philips Design, and as member of the Philips Design Board, he is responsible for both the strategic development of the global design function and the Design Research & Innovation program. In his role as strategist, he has been instrumental in transforming Philips Design from a service unit into a global function. The Design Research & Innovation program creates new design competences, future visions and new propositions for Philips, and has won numerous awards. The drive in the program is to create meaningful and relevant propositions based on a solid understanding of how these will evolve in the future, while ensuring that the propositions that land in the various business sectors increase the overall hit rate of Philips innovations.

In his professional career at Philips Design, Paul has worked in many different areas ranging from product, multimedia and Internet design to management and development roles. He is, and has been, a member of various boards, and juror for multiple renowned design competitions. He is also a frequent speaker at international design and innovation conferences. Paul studied industrial design engineering at Delft University of Technology, and holds a PhD in Design Innovation from the Eindhoven University of Technology.

References

Calabretta, G., and Gemser, G., 2015.
Integrating Design into the Fuzzy Front
End of the Innovation Process, PDMA's
Essentials 2: Design and Design Thinking.
John Wiley and Sons, New York.

Calabretta, G. and Perez, M. (2014). Can
you get smart in five days?, Crisp #3:
Fake it make it (pp. 10-13).

Gardien, P., Rincker, M., and Deckers,
E. (2016). Designing for the Knowledge
Economy: Accelerating Breakthrough
Innovation Through Co-creation. The
Design Journal, 19(2), 283-299.

PART II

Configuring a strategic design project

Shared
Vision

Ownership

03

MERIJN HILLEN
Fabrique

JEROEN VAN ERP
Fabrique

GIULIA CALABRETTA
Delft University of Technology

Designing Transitions: Pivoting Complex Innovation

3.1

Introduction

In 2014, the Rijksstudio – a platform within the website of the Holland's national Rijksmuseum where artworks from the collection are visualized in high resolution and in a Pinterest-like fashion – won 7 international design awards. Within three months of its official launch, this unique, interactive web platform had attracted more than 100,000 visits by people wishing to view, examine and curate their personal collections of over 200,000 masterpieces. This was a feat that not even the Google Art project – a well-known website with similar features – had accomplished in the 3 years it had been live.

Today, members of the Rijksstudio community have created more than 250,000 personal collections, and that number continues to rise. Rijksstudio's recipe for success is a perfect blend of viability (fit with the brand strategy), desirability (user-driven visual and interaction design) and feasibility (understanding of technological readiness). The Rijksstudio platform was developed by Fabrique, a strategic design agency with a strong focus on developing meaningful digital services. Hoping to achieve the same successful results,

museums from all over the world asked Fabrique to create a 'Rijksstudio' for their collections.

While these museums had assumed it was Fabrique's design knowledge and skills that would guarantee their success, they were quite surprised when Fabrique began by asking strategic questions related to their vision, values and organizational commitment. Here was the main take-away from the Rijksmuseum project – the dominant success factor of the Rijksstudio was not so much its design, as it was the great synergy between the museum's disrupting vision, the project owners' commitment and the designers' ability to facilitate coherent, brave choices throughout the project. It was that specific match-up of context and design leadership that had channelled the project's complexity – a number of different stakeholders, the need for coherence across several touchpoints, the novelty of the idea within the industry – into an appropriate design. Such an intangible mixture of skills cannot just be copy-pasted from museum to museum. We call the ability to create this mix 'Designing Transition' – recognize the complexity of the context, understand its key elements and driving forces, choose a starting point and act on it in order to lead the organization towards effective outcomes. We regard being able to 'design transitions' a key leadership competence that design professionals should strengthen in order to streamline complex strategic design projects. While designers are mainly trained to design solutions,

there is immense value in learning how to handle the complex challenges that arise on the bumpy road toward an innovative end result.

How can designers predict whether – or when – a project might stumble due to complexity? How can designers recognize circumstantial archetypes and how to

handle them? What type of informal leadership style should designers choose in order to streamline the process and ensure the most effective outcomes? The following paragraphs will provide design professionals with practical guidance on growing their ability to design transitions, and excel in the strategic practice of 'simplifying'.

Shared
Vision

Ownership

3.2

Assessing the circumstances: shared vision and ownership

In this chapter, we identify two dominant factors that influence the success of strategic design projects: a shared vision for the project, and a clear sense of ownership within the organization running the project. Plotting these factors on a vertical and horizontal axis leads to four typical project circumstances that require varying degrees of design leadership in order to 'design transitions' (Figure 3.1). In the following paragraphs, we offer guidelines on how to detect these different circumstances, and how to lead a project accordingly.

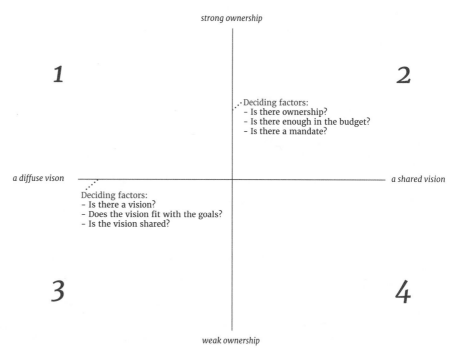

strong ownership

1

2

Deciding factors:
– Is there ownership?
– Is there enough in the budget?
– Is there a mandate?

a diffuse vison — — — — — — — — — — — — — a shared vision

Deciding factors:
– Is there a vision?
– Does the vision fit with the goals?
– Is the vision shared?

3

4

weak ownership

Figure 3.1: Assessing the circumstances

A shared vision
Making sure organizations and designers share the same vision is crucial to the success of any design project, and for innovation in general. A 'shared project vision' means there is widespread clarity in stakeholders' and designers' understanding of project goals and direction, and in the approach taken during project implementation. In addition, this shared vision includes a general coherence between the project vision and the overall vision of the organization (for more on this, please refer to Chapter 1).

The importance of sharing project vision
Having a clear and commonly shared vision is important for complex strategic design projects. The vision can align diverging perspectives and inform criteria used to make decisions – its unifying power is especially helpful when there are a variety of stakeholders, interests and interfaces involved in the design process.

Moreover, when the project's vision fits with the organization's brand strategy and overall vision, and when decision making at every level is a function of this vision, an organization's offering becomes a cohesive experience that is more appreciated by consumers (van Erp, 2011). Beyond this, a coherent vision nourishes the organization's internal culture and, subsequently the dedication and felt responsibility of company employees.

In small- and medium-sized organizations, operating in line with a clearly-defined, common vision is more of an exception than the status quo, and attuning the overall direction of innovation projects to a particular vision is not part of daily practice. Even larger organizations often fail to define and firmly embed a meaningful vision across the organization and its innovation projects. They rarely rely on a long-term perspective, and their innovation efforts are not guided by a pre-defined roadmap.

How to identify a shared vision
To decide what kind of leadership style is needed to 'design a transition', the design team needs to assess the extent to which the challenge at hand is driven by a vision that is shared. This can be done by asking three questions:

1. *Is there a project vision?* Does the company have a clear view of the project's direction, and where it fits into the *raison d'être* of the company? How exactly will the project help the company fulfil its *raison d'être*? A satisfactory answer to this question should emerge during the early stages of a strategic project, when the brief is formulated. In traditional design projects, briefs tend to be 'outcome-oriented' – they clearly indicate whether the outcome is a physical object or a service, and often include a precise description of the desired physical qualities of the design. In strategic projects, the brief must remain open in terms of the final design, and its definition should focus on understanding the motivation driving a project and the type of goals to be achieved. Lack of a clear-cut answer to these questions usually signals the absence of a strong, cohesive project vision.

2. *Is the project vision a good fit with the wider goals of the organization?* Sometimes the project vision does not align with the KPIs or primary goals that the organization has expressed elsewhere (for more on this, please refer to Chapter 7). This happens, for instance, when a trend emerges – organizations may act impulsively because they are afraid to miss out on what they see as an opportunity for growth.

3. *Is the vision shared across the company?* If there is a clear project vision, is there widespread awareness and alignment within the company? Can various departments move in the same direction during project setup and implementation?

Only if all three questions are answered positively can the project be plotted on the right side of the matrix.

Strong ownership
To appropriately align design leadership based on project circumstances, ownership is the second important factor to consider. Ownership refers to the extent to which there is a clear entity/department/stakeholder that initiates, finances and implements the strategic design project, and benefits from its outputs.

The importance of strong ownership
Most of strategic design project outcomes do not see the light of day, in many cases due to lack of ownership on the client side. Strong ownership of a project serves not only to focus the process of decision making *during* the project – more importantly, it secures a sustainable effect *once the project is completed*. A strategic outcome – a business opportunity, innovation portfolio or product/service system – is a continuum. Once it has been *installed*, it needs to be nurtured, developed and exploited. It needs ownership within a company. A strong sense of proprietorship gives organizational stakeholders the focus and drive to complete the project, despite complexity.

How to identify strong ownership
To evaluate the extent to which a strategic design process has a strong ownership within the organization, the design team should ask the following three questions:

1. *Who is responsible for the innovation project, its implementation and future nurturance?* Can the right person for the job, in terms of skills and position, already be found within the company? Is it a person who can also take care of implementing the project outcome? Does the right organizational structure exist to support ex-post nurturing? For instance, a project to develop a new e-commerce platform for an organization that has no online manager will not work in the long run. Projects need to be sustained and developed by individuals who have the power, drive and expertise needed to help the project grow.

2. *Does the project owner (or owner's department) hold the mandate to execute and complete the project?* Is the project owner able to take key project decisions independently, or does he/she always have to ask his/her manager? One of the biggest challenges in cutting through complexity is breaking down the silos and rigid hierarchies within an organization's infrastructure. A mandate from the board is one of the strongest weapons designers can use to combat this.

3. *Does the project owner (or owner's department) have a budget that matches the project's ambition and goals, and the implementation phase?* Enthusiasm is a key driver for innovation. It combines with optimism and a strong push from every stakeholder to get a project realized – but together with this enthusiasm comes the danger of losing sight of reality, and underestimating the time and money it takes to get the job done.

3.3

Four types of projects, four types of leadership

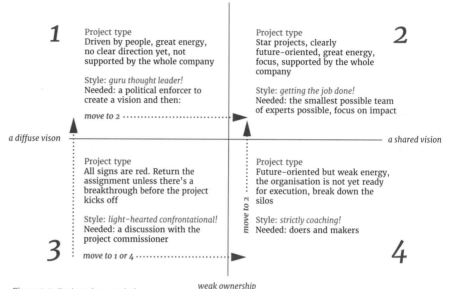

strong ownership

1

Project type
Driven by people, great energy, no clear direction yet, not supported by the whole company

Style: *guru thought leader!*
Needed: a political enforcer to create a vision and then:

move to 2 ....

2

Project type
Star projects, clearly future-oriented, great energy, focus, supported by the whole company

Style: *getting the job done!*
Needed: the smallest possible team of experts possible, focus on impact

a diffuse vison — *a shared vision*

Project type
All signs are red. Return the assignment unless there's a breakthrough before the project kicks off

Style: *light-hearted confrontational!*
Needed: a discussion with the project commissioner

3 *move to 1 or 4* ....

move to 2

Project type
Future-oriented but weak energy, the organisation is not yet ready for execution, break down the silos

Style: *strictly coaching!*
Needed: doers and makers

4

weak ownership

Figure 3.2: Project characteristics and leadership styles

Once the above questions have been answered, the big question becomes: *how to deal with the different circumstances?* Obviously it is a challenge to get real answers to the above questions on the table. For instance, the board often has a much more positive outlook when it comes to change processes than the organization's management and staff. Talking to multiple people and exploring previous project implementations might increase the reliability with which a designer can assess these two factors. Based on this assessment, each strategic design project can be plotted on the vision/ownership matrix, and designers can adjust their leadership accordingly (Figure 3.2).

In the following paragraphs, each typology is described and exemplified with a case from Fabrique's portfolio. A box at the beginning of each paragraph summarizes the characteristics of each typology.

Type 1 – The political enabler

This quadrant houses strategic design projects characterized by strong ownership and organizational support for innovation, but whose vision is diffused. These are projects where there are multiple ambitions to satisfy and differing opinions about which direction to take – resulting in the lack of a common, unifying vision, or in a vision that is an inappropriate fit for the desired goal. There is a need to combine different areas of expertise and a variety of departmental interests – often resulting in a state of overwhelming complexity that hinders the smooth and timely execution of the strategic design project.

In this context, design professionals can act as *political enablers*, by identifying the key objectives, key stakeholders and key expertise needed for the successful completion of the project, and facilitating their convergence towards a common vision. Convincing a client or an organization to rethink their vision is, in most cases, not very welcome news. The design team needs to act as a thoughtful, careful and trustworthy unit.

Figure 3.3: A screenshot of the Allerhande app

76

Case: Allerhande, a cooking app for Albert Heijn

Context

Albert Heijn – the Netherland's leading food retailer, and renowned for the momentum of their innovation – asked Fabrique to co-build a cooking app for Allerhande, one of their sub-brands. Since 1956, Albert Heijn has published a free print magazine about food and cooking, where the company's vision and brand statement is also broadcast clearly and distinctively. The magazine's role and purpose – its vision and branding attributes – were commonly understood and accepted across the company. At the start of this project, however, it became clear that there was no previously defined vision of the kind of digital experience they wanted the cooking app to deliver, and how the app would fit into the overarching company vision. Nevertheless, there was a great product owner who championed the project within the team and the entire organization, so much so that the whole design team was willing to exert extra effort and make it work.

Solution

Through a series of creative workshops with product owners, Albert Heijn and Allerhande brand managers and content managers from a media agency, Fabrique designers used their creative facilitation skills to collaboratively develop a solid project vision that defined where the product would go and how the team would get there. The team created an 'interaction vision' and a plan to implement an agile development environment within the company where all parties involved could better understand the vision and contribute to the app's development. The app was launched in October 2014, and became a huge success (see Figure 3.3). Thanks to the strong and coherent vision behind it, Albert Heijn has been able to maintain, nurture and develop the application as part of their customer touchpoint strategy.

Take-away

As the example shows, the team of designers played the role of *political enablers* by using creative facilitation techniques to distil a vision that united different parties and stakeholders within the company. There is no strict way to handle this. Designers could use vision creation tools like 'ViP' (Hekkert and Van Dijk, 2011; see also Chapter 1) or 'frame creation' (Dorst, 2015) to get key stakeholders around the table and moderate the discussion in a way that any conflicts of interest would be openly addressed and dissolved, which makes room for a common vision to emerge. In any situation, it's important to make sure the vision is shared by all the relevant people and departments in the company, since the designer's aim is to move to quadrant 2.

Type 2 – The excellent executor

Type 2 projects are the star projects. There is shared vision and ownership, what else could a designer wish for? This is the ideal starting point to be able to manage complexity and lead a strategic design process to successful completion. Indeed, the role of design leadership is limited to that of the *excellent executor* who takes care that the job is done in the most effective and efficient way, with the smallest, most appropriate team available. Methods like 'scrum' or 'rapid co-creation' (see Chapter 2) can help designers keep up the pace, the energy and the commitment needed to conduct this type of project.

Figure 3.4: A sketch of the 'e-gate' for Schipol Airport   **Figure 3.5:** Self-service border control in use

Case: Schiphol, self-service border control

Context

Every year, approximately 60 million passengers pass through the border control area at Schiphol airport in the Netherlands. Schiphol asked several agencies to participate in a pitch to 'Redesign the Passenger Process' (RPP). The goal of the project was simple – improve passenger flow. However, the context was highly complex, given the considerable number of stakeholders involved and the extreme rigidity in the regulations and bureaucracy that characterize the airport environment.

Solution

The designers at Fabrique realized that in order to address such complexity and win the pitch, a strong project vision that reflected the project goals was the way to go. The agency did some extensive research and rethinking around the domain of border control, and presented a clear vision showing how the project objectives could be achieved. Specifically, the agency concluded that border control was a bump in the overall flow of operations, and passengers' experiences were not very favorable – the border check felt more like an intimidating criminal search. Thus, their vision was to turn the border control into a warm, welcoming area that led to the duty-free shopping zone. The vision was immediately embraced by the airport and all of the other stakeholders. The RPP project was strongly supported by the entire organization, and eventually a special innovation taskforce – the airport, the architect, a wayfinding specialist, the Ministry of Justice and the border police – took ownership, with the intention, mandate and budget to support the project. Subsequently, the initial vision smoothly developed into a feasible outcome – the 'e-gate' (see Figure 3.4). At one point during project development, the Ministry of Justice realized that the innovative e-gate could be useful at various locations, not only at Schiphol. They took over the project, and 5 years after the first ideas were generated, the first real e-gates were installed at Schiphol Airport. Nowadays you can find them all over the world (see Figure 3.5).

Take-away

The rapid and successful conclusion of the e-gate project showcases the importance of establishing both a commonly shared vision and clear ownership from the outset of a project. The vision articulated in the process was smoothly executed thanks to a small, dedicated expert team that was selected to get the job done. The team had the courage to make fast, risky decisions, despite the complexity of the airport ecosystem.

Main characteristics of the light-hearted confrontational leader

Characteristics: weak ownership / diffuse vision

Main challenges: all signs are red / overwhelming complexity

Leadership goals: breakthrough in circumstances to move the project towards quadrant 1 or 4

Needed team members: persistent leader, with light-hearted confrontational skills and mandate to return the assignment if needed

Type 3 – The light-hearted, confrontational leader

This typology is exactly the opposite of the one described in the previous paragraph. There is no real sense that the complexity of the project can be resolved and the project will be a success. A design professional usually gets into a situation like this when the project commissioner is unaware of the situation he or she is in. Designers will need to identify this kind of situation as quickly as possible, and broach the topic with stakeholders immediately. Indicators are: indecisiveness relative to project start and execution timelines, spending project budget without achieving results due to unrestrained processes, or – in the case of external assignments – the fact that the tender has existed for a considerable amount of time without being assigned to any agency. This situation might also occur when an ambitious new director has been appointed. A 'shot from the hip' – which he or she calls the vision – and a lack of awareness about the structure of the organization will likely increase the chances of failure. A light-hearted, confrontational leadership style – and potentially an initial refusal to undertake the assignment – is the best way to confront a commissioner with this situation. Once the problem and its causes are known to both parties, designers should use their leadership to move the project towards quadrant 1 by creating ownership – assigning responsibility, obtaining a mandate, agreeing on a budget – or towards quadrant 4, by supporting the organization's efforts to develop a vision that everyone shares. The latter approach is closer to the designer's core set of competencies, and thus a better starting point – rather than attempting to change the organizational structure to create ownership.

Case: Creating a brand new museum in the Netherlands – the National Military Museum

Context

In many ways, the National Military Museum (NMM) is a one-of-a-kind project. The idea was to merge two Dutch military museums into one larger museum, and install the merged entity in a newly-designed building on the former military airbase at Soesterberg in the Netherlands. The merged museum would be one of a group of four National Defence museums, which also included the Navy Museum, Military Police Museum and Special Forces Museum. The project was one of the Netherlands' first public tenders to experiment with handing over the realization and exploitation of a public cultural heritage institution to the private sector for 25 years. Heijmans, a large construction company, was the main contractor for the tender, and would lead a consortium of landscape and exhibition architects, installers, exploitation companies and different creative agencies. Fabrique was asked to take care of digital interactions. Despite the high level of motivation, none of the parties had experience executing such a project. Thus, both a common vision and clear ownership were absent, and most parties – including the project leader – had no inkling of their position and role. The risk of failure was high.

Solution

Heijmans was aware that it was lacking in expertise, as the construction company had never created educational content for a museum, never worried about developing a new digital interaction, and never had to take care of a business case for a restaurant. Heijmans got all the creative agencies involved in the plans for the museum at an early stage, and 'outsourced' the creation of the vision(s) to each of them, including the smaller areas, according to their field of expertise. When Fabrique designers got the assignment to develop a vision for the museum's digital experience, their reaction was firm – they demanded the opportunity to develop the branding and visual identity for the project, and the overall branding for the other Dutch Defence museums. Over the course of several discussions and confrontational meetings, Fabrique steered Heijmans towards accepting a single, solid structure for the Dutch Defence Musea brand, which included the NMM and the three other brands for the different military museums (see Figure 3.6). As part of its confrontational leadership style, Fabrique also pushed for the allocation of a specific budget dedicated to creating the brand vision, which had not been included in the initial tender. Their actions also served to cement ownership for the project, and paved the way for commitment to the approach until the final stages of its implementation.

Figure 3.6: The new visual identity for NMM

Take-away

In type 3 projects, there is a high risk of project failure. The NMM case shows however, that catastrophe can be warded off by developing awareness of the circumstances and eventual need to confer responsibility onto those with greater expertise. Being brave enough to perceive professional shortcomings and confront clients/stakeholders is the most essential part of moving a type 3 project into a type 2 or 4. This skill therefore asks for a senior designer who shows authority and has excellent reflective and confrontational skills.

Type 4 – The coaching leader

In this quadrant there is a clear vision. However, although the direction the innovation needs to take may be evident, the organization is not ready for it. There is no ownership, there is often no budget and the organization is unaware of or does not have enough ambition to implement new products and/or services. Thus, the complexity resides in the implementation, rather than in the conception of the design. The type of leadership that design professionals can employ to simplify this kind of process consists of coaching organizations in project implementation, which progressively creates ownership. Thus, design professionals should take the lead in executing the project according to the vision, and at the same time teach the organization the necessary tools, methods and principles (for more on this, please refer to Chapter 8). The vision acts as a driving force for creating ownership.

Case: Agra city branding

Archohm is an architectural agency in Noida, close to Delhi, India. The agency was commissioned by the city of Agra to design a new tourism infrastructure for the city. The aim was not only to position the Taj Mahal as the main attraction in the area, but also to make clear that Agra has much more to offer. The architects felt that the city needed to tell a clear story, and their vision was to position the city itself as a brand. They found inspiration in cities that make use of strong branding statements like 'I Love NY', 'Copenhagen' and 'I amsterdam'. The municipality of Agra could not imagine how this could be achieved, and what the effect would be. The architects were not able to find ownership.

Solution

The lack of ownership was attributed to the fact that the people at the municipality were not familiar with the phenomenon of city branding, its benefits and how to go about doing it. The architects had two options – scout for an owner within the municipality, or take a design approach and create ownership by co-developing a brand concept with key stakeholders to stoke the fires under the project. They opted for the latter, and gave the design agency the lead in co-designing the project concept. Together with Archohm, the designers developed an initial concept and a few manifestations for the new brand (see Figure 3.7). These were presented to the Chief Ministers of Uttar Pradesh and the City of Agra, who were quite surprised by the impact. The initial concept and the designs bolstered the process. All the stakeholders in the city embraced the concept presented. The head of tourism

Figure 3.7: An example of Agra city branding

became the owner of the project. The lack of ownership was resolved through the co-creative and coaching approach utilized by the design agency. The city commissioned the architect and design agencies for the full development of the city brand, and today the concept and the designs are implemented in Agra, which is home to the Taj Mahal.

Take-away
When using a coaching leadership style, co-creation tools can help to instil a sense of proprietorship and boost project development. Methods like 'scrum' and a solid presence within the organization can get the project rolling. In this case, a scrum master from the design agency, with clear targets in mind, was able to perform miracles in terms of the execution of the overall process. And the existence of a solid vision helped to accelerate the process – a strong vision empowers ownership.

3.4

Conclusion

While working on complex projects, a large part of the complexity lies in the dynamics that propel the process towards a valuable outcome. Therefore, we strongly believe that, for strategic designers, being willing to 'get things done' is as important as creating a great design. In this chapter, we have shown that there are two major influences on the agility of the process: a solid project vision and the degree of ownership within the organization. The extent to which these two factors occur help designers determine what leadership role to take on in order to move the project forward. However, it would be far too easy to conclude that projects that establish a common vision and great ownership all have a chance of 'winning', whilst projects lacking these things will automatically be fraught with problems

– unmet targets, budgetary overruns, not to mention human frustration. Although it might seem obvious to consider the circumstances as indicators for success, we advise you not to see them as such. There is more.

Projects with a sound vision and clear ownership could turn out to be rather dull, leading to poorly-motivated team members and mediocre outcomes. On the other hand, introducing an innovative idea into projects lacking in ownership can attract and motivate the right owners, and ensure the project gets off the ground, as in the case of the National Military Museum. These examples show that motivation and novelty – among other factors – can be of considerable influence as well. Other project indicators – such as garnering the support of top management for the project leader/owner, or mixing up the composition of the project team – might also be considered. In addition to assessing project circumstances, we strongly believe that self-reflection and assessment are equally important. Design professionals should get to know their strengths and weaknesses – and this knowledge should guide their choice of projects so that their unique combination of skills and expertise can help them lead the effort to 'get things done'. Design professionals should ask themselves questions like:

Am I someone who likes to lead the way through complex politics? Am I a strong vision creator, or am I actually more of an executor who excels in specific areas of expertise, and who needs to be surrounded by strong team members? Do I need to agree with the vision, or does agreement make no difference to me?

Connecting circumstances to the people that actually excel under those circumstances will put design teams in the best starting position. That moment of self-reflection is ultimately something all designers are responsible for – a moment when they consciously decide whether to refuse the project, locate the right team members or just move forward.

Constantly changing roads

And if the decision is to move forward, it is also important to keep in mind that people change, and circumstances change. Showing leadership is not only a matter of choosing a style but also maintaining a delicate balance.

Designers have to keep a broader perspective of the project and make sure the design team's ambition does not wane. This means listening, as well as showing the way. Designers need to lead *and* be humble at same time. By taking responsibility for the route, and not merely targeting the final destination, designers will work more intimately with their clients – which means nurturing a productive relationship, rather than presenting completed work now and then.

We believe that the central responsibility of the designer is to respect and produce a desired impact, and that designing the road is as important as the design itself. And once designers master this, they might find out how enjoyable and rewarding the strategic design process can be.

MERIJN HILLEN works as a creative strategist focusing on brand driven innovation at design agency Fabrique. She has over ten years experience assisting clients with their business transformations. By connecting organizational purpose and business strategy to consumer insights and zeitgeist, she aims to create new (digital) products, services and communications that are meaningful, positive and profitable. Merijn studied Industrial Design Engineering at Delft University of Technology (MSc), and branding at the European Institute of Brand Management, Rotterdam. She contributed to the Creative Industry Scientific Program (CRISP), which focused on stimulating the continuing growth of the Dutch Design Sector and Creative Industries. She is currently involved in the development of a new master's program in Digital Design at the HvA (Amsterdam University of Applied Sciences), and is an occasional coach at the faculty of Industrial Design Engineering at Delft University of Technology. Her publications on design and innovation and her personal writings can be found on Medium.

JEROEN VAN ERP graduated from the Faculty of Industrial Design Engineering at Delft University of Technology in 1988. In 1992, he was one of the founders of the multidisciplinary design bureau Fabrique. In 1994, he established Fabrique's interactive media department, whose focus on website development was extremely novel at the time. Under Jeroen's joint leadership, Fabrique has grown through the years into a multifaceted design consultancy. It currently employs more than 100 artists, engineers and storytellers working for a wide range of customers. Fabrique is one of the leading companies in the field of design in the Netherlands. Jeroen is currently innovation strategist at Fabrique. He is also a guest lecturer for various courses, a board member of the BNO, the Dutch Designers Association, and chair of the Dutch Creative Council. From 2012 to 2016 he was a member of Topteam Creative Industries. In this role, together with his colleagues, he was responsible for guiding the international ambitions of the creative sector. In November 2015, he was appointed professor of concept design at the Faculty of Industrial Design Engineering at Delft University of Technology.

GIULIA CALABRETTA is Associate Professor of the Strategic Value of Design at the Faculty of Industrial Design Engineering, Delft University of Technology. Giulia received a Master's Degree in Management and Marketing from Bocconi University (Italy). She also holds a PhD in Management Science from ESADE Business School (Spain), and a Post Doc from BI Norwegian School of Management (Norway). Giulia believes that using design and design practices is the best way for companies to become more innovative in nature and structure, and will prepare them to embrace the behavioural, technological and cultural revolutions of the future. Her current research focus is on understanding how design practices and capabilities can be effectively and permanently integrated into a company's innovation strategy and processes. Additionally, she is interested in what makes a great Chief Design Officer, and why each company (and institution) should have one. Her research has been published in such journals as *Organization Studies*, *Journal of Product Innovation Management*, *Journal of Business Ethics*, *Journal of Service Theory* and *Practice*, *Journal of Service Management*.

References

Dorst, K. (2015). *Frame innovation: Create new thinking by design*. MIT Press.

Hekkert, P., and Van Dijk, M. (2011). *ViP–Vision in Design: A Guidebook for Innovators*. BIS Publishers.

Verganti, R. (2008). Design, meanings, and radical innovation: A metamodel and a research agenda*. *Journal of Product Innovation Management*, 25(5), 436–456.

Perks, H., Cooper, R., and Jones, C. (2005). Characterizing the Role of Design in New Product Development: An Empirically Derived Taxonomy*. *Journal of Product Innovation Management*, 22(2), 111–127.

Van Erp, J. (2011). Designing the Total Experience in Diversity and Unity, proceedings of IASDR 2011, the 4th World Conference on Design Research, Delft / NL.

KASIA TABEAU
Erasmus University Rotterdam

GERDA GEMSER
RMIT University

JOS OBERDORF
npk design

Creating Process Understanding: Design Practices and Abilities

Introduction

Strategic design projects involve problems that are often poorly defined and highly complex (Duck, 2012). Because these projects focus on shaping the future (Golsby-Smith, 2007), the relative uncertainty of their outcomes may clash with the risk-averse nature of most organizations and their management. An approach for designers to reduce this uncertainty is to carefully and consciously establish *process understanding.* Creating process understanding means explaining or even teaching organizational stakeholders how the design process works. The skills deployed by designers and the practices they engage in (their ways of working) are very different to the conventional working methods that most organizations are familiar with. To create understanding of the design process, designers need to clearly define what the different steps and activities they engage in entail, and demonstrate how they expect to bring about outcomes.

In this chapter, we report our findings from a study of the working methods of Dutch design consultancy *npk design*, to illustrate the kinds of practices that help designers to create process understanding. *npk design* is a recognized Dutch design consultancy that manages the entire development process from strategy and ideation to engineering, prototyping and production support. We present, in depth, two innovation projects that were completed by this design agency (See boxes 1 and 2).

npk design divides the innovation process into three phases: strategy, design and realization. The strategy phase focuses on defining the problem that will be

solved in the project as well as exploring the context in which the solution for that problem will be introduced. The strategy phase ends with a design brief that describes the solution space. Ideas for the solution are developed in the design phase, after which a selected idea is prototyped, tested and engineered.

Finally, in the realization phase, the engineered solution is produced. In this final phase, *npk design* guides the production of the solution developed for its organizations. The role of *npk design* in realizing the solution ends when the first series of the solution is delivered.

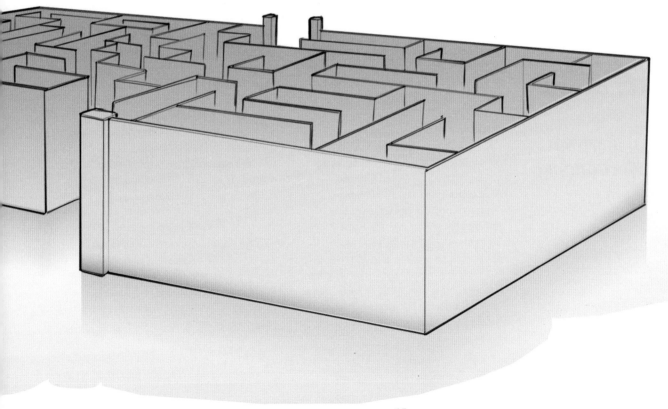

4.2

Practices supporting process understanding

To help organizations understand the design process, designers at *npk design* use six main practices. Table 4.1 shows these six practices and their definitions. We will discuss how the designers at *npk design* use the six practices during the innovation process (see also Figure 4.1).

Designers can create process understanding by *making the process accountable*. Accountability is achieved by standardizing, formalizing and documenting the design process. Contracts can formalize the process, Information and Communication Technology (ICT) can be used to document and track it, and adhering to an ISO standard throughout will strengthen it. Creating accountability is particularly important during the strategy phase, when the contract is being drafted.

Designers should not only specify the tasks to be executed, but also be clear about what they are *not* going to do during the design process. Demonstrating process accountability is also important at the end of the other two phases (design and realization), in the interest of maintaining communication and demonstrating process integrity. Carefully documenting the process, from beginning to end, helps designers explain why certain decisions were made at certain times.

The second practice is to *make the process tangible* through representations that visibly explain the process and clarify how it will evolve. Designers achieve this by making drawings and flow charts of the process (Figure 4.2 is an example), by explaining the process

Table 4.1: Design practices for process understanding

Practice	Definition	Actions designers can take
Make the process accountable	Designers' efforts to standardize, formalise and document the design process, to cement agreement with organizations regarding the actions to be taken, or not taken, throughout.	· Use contracts · Use ICT to document and track the process · Work to an ISO standard
Make the process tangible	Designers' efforts to create visual representations of the process, for the purposes of explaining and clarifying the process to organizations, and providing an example of what this process will look like for the project in question.	· Make flowcharts of the process · Describe the process used in previous projects · Make a video that depicts the process
Synchronize designers' and organizations' processes	Designers' and organizations' efforts to continuously share their progress with each other, to ensure that they are moving toward a common outcome at a similar pace, and using similar actions.	· Use the cloud to collaborate · Make and regularly update project plans · Maintain frequent contact (email, phone, meetings)
Instil process ownership	Designers' efforts to shape the process according to organizations' preferences, to ensure that they consider it 'their own', support it fully, and are willing to follow it.	· Use organizational information to shape the process · Allow organizations to make decisions and give feedback about the process · Monitor satisfaction
Bring the results of the process to life	Designers' efforts to create tangible visual representations of the outcome, in order to reach agreement with organizations about what is going to be developed during the process, as well as to demonstrate that the process is appropriate.	· Use drawings, and 2D and 3D visualizations · Illustrate the solution in context through film or photography · Let organizations engage with the solution in product tests
Acclimate organizations to designers' ways of working	Designers' efforts in actively involving organizations in designerly activities to let them understand the process and to let them gain empathy for designers and their work.	· Make organization members part of the design team · Let organizations design (sketch, make models, etc.) · Involve organizations in user research

followed in previous projects and by making movies about various parts of the process (e.g., user research, concept generation). Making the process tangible is important in the strategy phase when essential decisions are made about the process. A tangible representation of this process can, for example, clarify the consequences of choices. Making the process tangible also helps designers educate organizations unfamiliar with the strategic design process about the phases and steps it comprises. As noted by an *npk* designer: 'A lot of organizations do not think in terms of a process with steps that have to be taken. They see it as one big thing (...) So I am teaching them how design works'. Educating organizations by making the process tangible is important not only at the beginning of the project, during the strategy phase, but also at the start of the other phases (design and realization), because visual representations serve as timely reminders about what is going to happen in the next phase, and cement connections with earlier phases.

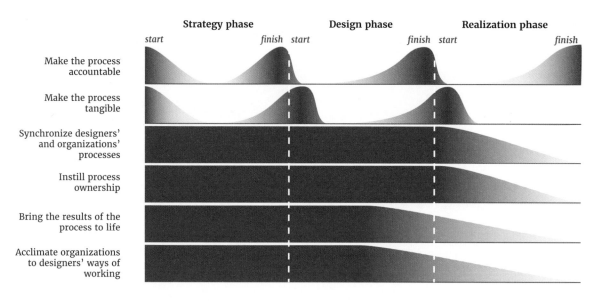

Figure 4.1: Practices in use during the strategy, design and realization phases

To further teach and generate process understanding, the designers at *npk design* also *synchronize designers' and organizations' processes,* which involves continuously sharing progress updates so that the design consultancy and the organization move towards the same outcome at the same pace, and use similar methods. Making and updating project plans, and maintaining frequent contact through email, phone and meetings are examples of actions that designers can take. Synchronizing processes is important at the beginning, in the strategy phase, to understand what kind of approach is most conducive to organizational cooperation. As one *npk* designer put it, 'What you often see is that it is about matching organizations. How do we work, how do you work? Can we find a format that fits?'. Maintaining this synchronized approach is, however, also important in the design and realization phases, because it guarantees that everyone remains aware of the actions taken or needed to reach the project's outcome. Continuous alignment is made easy by the use of the latest ICT tools and techniques, such as cloud-based file sharing.

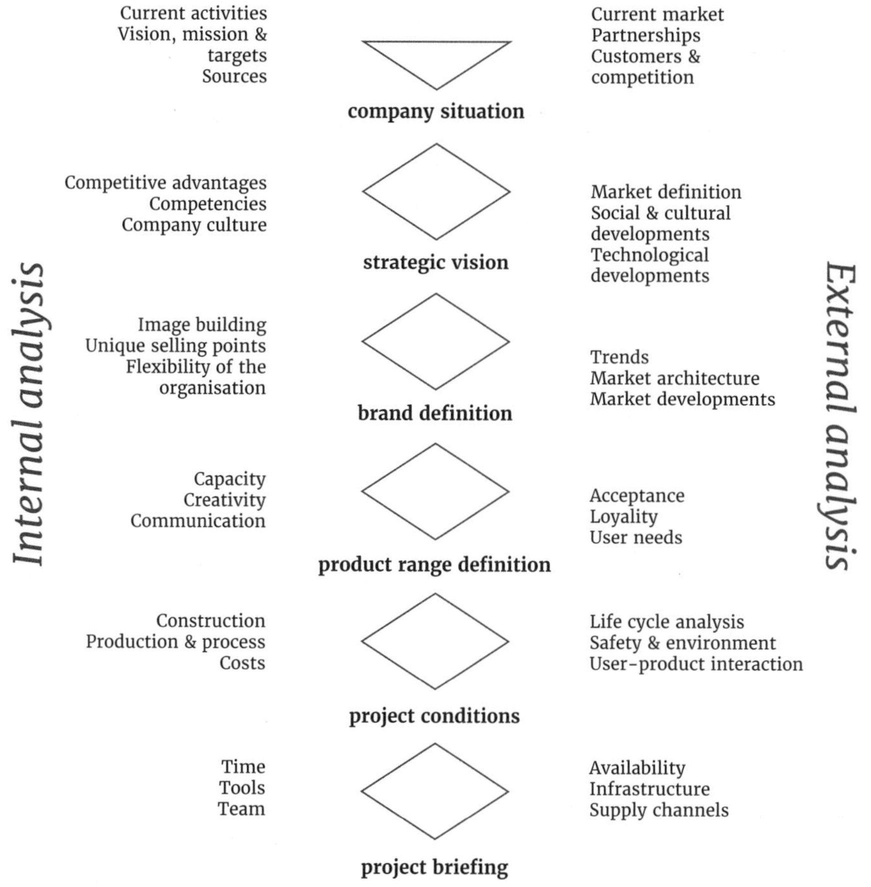

Internal analysis

External analysis

Current activities
Vision, mission &
targets
Sources

company situation

Current market
Partnerships
Customers &
competition

Competitive advantages
Competencies
Company culture

strategic vision

Market definition
Social & cultural
developments
Technological
developments

Image building
Unique selling points
Flexibility of the
organisation

brand definition

Trends
Market architecture
Market developments

Capacity
Creativity
Communication

product range definition

Acceptance
Loyality
User needs

Construction
Production & process
Costs

project conditions

Life cycle analysis
Safety & environment
User–product interaction

Time
Tools
Team

project briefing

Availability
Infrastructure
Supply channels

Figure 4.2: A flowchart that makes the process tangible

The fourth practice involved in process understanding is _instilling ownership for the process_, which relates to designers' efforts to shape the process in a way that respects preferences of the organization. Instilling ownership ensures that the organization will consider the process its own, support it, and be willing to follow it (see also Chapter 3). This practice involves actions such as letting organizations make decisions about and give feedback on the process, and monitoring their satisfaction. Instilling ownership for the process is important during all three phases, but particularly during the strategy and design phases. During the strategy phase, organizations can be involved in decisions about what the process will look like, while during the design phase they can be invited to give feedback on every step of the idea generation process, and hence influence any further action that is taken. Continuous managing and monitoring of an organization's satisfaction ensures satisfaction with the process and outcomes ('With every step that we take, we ask "Are you happy? Or not?" We do this to avoid taking one step forward and two steps back').

The fifth practice, *bringing the result of the process to life*, relates to designers' efforts to create visual and tangible representations of (interim) outcomes; for example, using drawings, visualizing the solution with 2D and 3D tools, showing the solution in context through film or photography or letting organizations engage with the solution in product tests. At the beginning of the project, during the strategy phase, it is important to bring the solution spaces of the process to life, so that everybody is on the same page regarding the direction to be taken and what actions are required. An example of a drawing that was used by *npk design* for this purpose is shown in Figure 4.3. This drawing leaves plenty of room for interpretation, but helped the designers to discuss project direction with the organization and the kind of process required to 'make it happen'. Bringing solution spaces to life is clearly important during the design phase, when product or service concepts are being developed. Towards the end of the design phase, when the solution has largely taken shape, bringing the end solution to life through film and photography can help the organization visualize it in its context. All these actions enhance organizations' understanding of the process – and the outcome – by providing 'proof' that the proposed process is 'delivering results'.

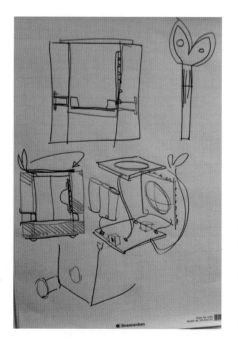

The final practice that designers use to create process understanding is *acclimating organizations to designerly ways of working*, which means actively involving organizations in the design process to enable them not only to understand it, but also to develop empathy for designers and their activities. Examples of this practice include making the organization part of the design team, letting them sketch or make models and prototypes, or engaging them in ethnographic research.

Getting organizations accustomed to designerly ways of working is valuable in the strategy phase, and even more so in the design phase, since organizations often do not understand the uncertainty and 'messiness' associated with these phases. Making the organization part of the design team can attenuate this problem, as the organization will experience first-hand the 'messiness' and uncertainty ('I involve them [organizations], so that they feel that it is not easy. Sometimes things remain unsolved. And when they are part of the process they understand this much better'). Moreover, by letting organizations sketch out their own ideas, they are better able to assess the quality of these ideas ('We make the client sketch. (...) When something is in your head, you think that it's a great idea! [...] Until you start drawing, and then you think, "Oh no, that's not it!"'). Towards the end of the design phase, the end solution has largely taken shape, after which letting organizations experience designerly ways of working becomes less relevant.

Figure 4.3: Bringing the result of the process to life with a drawing

4.3

Abilities needed to support process understanding

Table 4.2 lists and defines the six abilities that support designers who wish to create and improve organizations' process understanding. These abilities may be relevant to different practices. However, in Table 4.2, we identify the practice for which an ability is of particular relevance.

The first important skill that supports process understanding is the *ability to oversee the process.* A strategic design process encompasses a wide variety of interrelated elements – creative, temporal, legal, financial – all of which need to be accounted for ('More and more aspects come together...more elements that you have to do magic with to make sure the process goes smoothly'). Overseeing the process includes keeping track of whether the process is proceeding according to plan – on time and on budget – a skill that can only really be acquired after years of practice. Even though every member of the design team typically receives a steady stream of information, only an experienced designer is able to tie all that information together and follow it up with concrete, process-related activities. A junior designer tends to think in terms of outcomes, and not in terms of the formalities required to eventually achieve those outcomes ('You could say that this is very close to a stage-gate kind of approach – which documents do I need to have signed, sealed and delivered to go forward?'). Designers must also be able to 'translate' different types of information into a 'language' that ties the process and its progress directly to organizational imperatives and benchmarks ('You have to translate your results, intermediate results, into a bookkeeping language to make it accountable').

Table 4.2: Design abilities for process understanding

Ability	Definition	Supports designers in:
Oversee the process	Designers' ability to perceive the overall progress of the process, by interpreting and integrating any activity carried out, and documenting these in a rational, formalized way.	Making the process accountable
Steer the process forward	Designers' ability to make stakeholders adhere to the process by showing mastery of the process, and by explaining and clarifying it in terms the organization understands and knows.	Making the process tangible
Adjust the process iteratively	Designers' ability to align their and the organizations' activities and expectations on a continuous basis.	Synchronizing the designers' and organizations' processes
Connect with organizations	Designers' ability to both sense what kind of organization they are working with, what its needs are, and how these needs change over time; and to use this empathic input to shape the process in a way that is appropriate.	Instilling process ownership
Tell a coherent and compelling story	Designers' ability to integrate the activities undertaken during the process into a narrative that brings the result of the process to life and illustrates the relevance of the process to follow.	Bringing the result of the process to life
Create engagement	Designers' ability to stimulate organizations' emotional and cognitive interaction with the process.	Acclimating the organization to designerly ways of working

Steering the process forward, the second important skill that contributes to process understanding, implies that the designer has mastered the design process to such an extent that he or she can *compel* stakeholders to adhere to it and to ratify decisions the designer makes. Mastering the process involves not only an in-depth understanding of what a design process entails, but also an ability to adapt that understanding to the specific project in question ('I know what my idea of the process is. But I have to develop a new story for every project'). To explain and obtain ratification for the process, designers need to be able to demonstrate the process visually ('Often you have to visualize, or verbally spell out the steps you are going to take and why. Just having them in your head is not enough'). Designers also need to be able to tell a convincing story based on prior experience ('You tell your story, and you build up credibility. You say, "It worked there, so we are also going to do it like this", or the other way around, "It didn't work there, so we are not going to do it for this and this reason"').

Demonstrating the ability to *adjust the process iteratively* means continuously aligning designerly activities and expectations with those of organizations, so that everyone moves through the process at the same speed toward the same solution. To align actions and expectations, designers hold regular, formal meetings to communicate the status of the process, and determine – together with organizations – the next steps to be undertaken. These meetings are also an opportunity for designers to (re)explain and adjust the solution space so that it is in line with organizations' wishes. To ensure that processes and outcomes are aligned, it is important that designers adopt an 'analytical frame of mind', and ask themselves how to adjust the process and solution spaces in ways that take the specifics of the project into account rather than operating based on past experience alone.

Having the ability to *connect with organizations* means being able to sense the kind of organization the client represents, what their needs are and how those needs change over time, and to use this empathic input to shape the process in a way that is appropriate. Demonstrating this kind of empathy helps organizations feel like they have ownership over the process. Another way to ensure that organizations perceive the process as their own, and are willing to follow it, is to establish a personal relationship with them. The close involvement fostered by a personal relationship makes it easier for designers to uncover the (deeper) motives behind the project, and shape the process accordingly. Having the ear of the organization means that designers may even be given some leeway to fix any mistakes they make ('If you have a connection with the client, he will give you the space to correct things, "You screwed up and you have the opportunity to make it right"').

An ability to *create a coherent and compelling story* enables designers to weave a narrative that simultaneously brings the results of the process to life and demonstrates the relevance of the process to be followed. Often, the narrative is constructed together with the organization. To begin, designers propose 'a storyline' that 'grabs' stakeholders' attention, which is further developed in tandem with the organization. That story sets the stage for the process to be followed. Indeed, any process-related decisions designers make should be traced back to the story, to maintain narrative – and hence procedural – integrity. In addition, solution spaces should naturally 'follow the storyline'. When developing narratives, designers need to take different stakeholder interests into account, and make sure that all the puzzle pieces fall into place, which makes the storyline far more convincing.

The last ability, that is, the *ability to create engagement*, relates to designers' ability to get organizations involved with the process cognitively *and* emotionally. This level of engagement is generated by engineering positive experiences. For example, designers can transform the process into a show or a play, 'To boost that enthusiasm, make sure it is a party'. Engagement also involves making organizations feel that they are really part of the process ('They become members of the team, and they move in with you, so to speak. They sleep under your desk'). Client engagement almost always ensures that organizations will commit to the process and its outcomes, so designers need to have the ability to convince and generate enthusiasm at the right time ('During the presentation, you often have one opportunity to give your arguments, about why it is a good solution, [and you should do so] in a solid way. You should grab the opportunity'). To motivate engagement, designers can actively involve organizations when identifying the problem and solution spaces ('They start to think along with us'), which enables organizations to get accustomed to how designers work as well.

4.4

Case studies

This section provides an overview of the design practices and abilities used in two separate projects conducted by npk design.

The Bike Accessory project

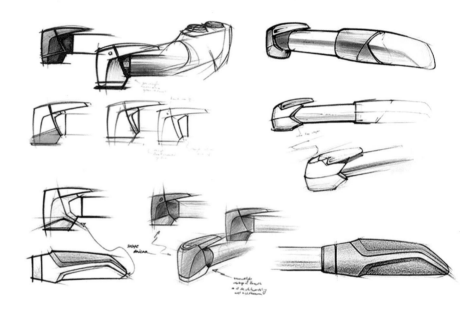

Client

SKS Germany is a manufacturer of bike accessories based in Sunder, Germany. SKS Germany develops and sells products such as bicycle mini-pumps and frame pumps, mudguards, chain guards, tools, bags, bottles and bottle holders. The company aims mainly at the high end of the market, with a focus on both functionality and design. The company has an in-house research and development department, and its own production plants.

Initiation

SKS Germany contacted *npk design* to develop style guides for each of its products. However, it was also looking for a long-term design partner for its new product development initiatives. Building a relationship meant that SKS Germany needed to understand the design process that *npk design* follows, so creating process understanding was an important component of the project. SKS Germany involved *npk design* in the strategy and design phase; *npk design* was not involved in the realization phase.

Strategy phase

In the strategy phase, *npk design* conducted three portfolio management workshops alongside representatives from SKS Germany. These workshops were not only designed to develop style guides for SKS Germany (as per the original assignment), they also enabled a broader evaluation of SKS Germany's product portfolio. The workshops helped SKS Germany and *npk design* to assess each other's expectations and capabilities. The strategy phase began with an investigation of competing products on the market and SKS Germany's current portfolio. The results became part of the first workshop. This first workshop led to the insight that SKS Germany's portfolio should be structured in accordance with its target markets. *npk design* created three personas to represent SKS Germany's target markets. These personas were presented and discussed during the second joint workshop, and the subsequent style guides were created for these personas. In the third workshop, priorities for product development were determined, based on whether SKS Germany 's existing products were suited to the defined target markets and personas. On the basis of this evaluation, two initiatives were selected for the design phase: the development of a high-end and a low-end mini-bicycle pump to cover the broad spectrum of design styles represented in the portfolio of SKS Germany.

Design phase

In the design phase, the two mini-bicycle pumps and style guides were developed. The designers of *npk design* developed ideas and concepts, and presented these outcomes to SKS Germany over the course of several meetings. In these meetings, 2D and 3D visualizations were used to show both the interim outcomes and the process through which these interim outcomes emerged. SKS Germany provided feedback on the interim outcomes, and decided which outcomes to continue with, and which to set aside. The concepts selected were drawn in detail by the designers of *npk design* using CAD/CAM software, and at the end of the design phase *npk design* handed over the files to SKS Germany. As a last step, the initial style guides were adjusted based on the insights from the design phase.

Realization phase

SKS Germany was responsible for realizing the concepts. The files they received from *npk design* detailed the outer shape of the bicycle pumps: the inside of the pumps was detailed by the engineers of SKS Germany. Hereafter, the bicycle pumps were taken into production, which was also handled by SKS Germany.

After the project

npk design became the long-term partner of SKS Germany for its product development initiatives. After the two bicycle pumps, more projects followed that focused on restructuring the portfolio of SKS Germany as evaluated in the workshops.

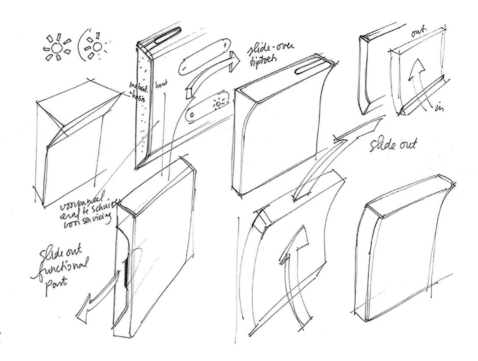

The Cloud heater project

Client
Nerdalize is a provider of computing power services to both industry and academia based in Delft, the Netherlands. The organization was founded in 2013 by three entrepreneurs with the vision of creating a world in which heating is free, and computing power an affordable commodity.

Initiation
When Nerdalize contacted *npk design*, it was still in its start-up phase, trying to sell affordable computing power by installing servers in consumers' houses. The project Nerdalize wanted to initiate with *npk design* focused on developing a heater in which the servers could be placed. *npk design* suggested that developing this heater would not be enough to help Nerdalize set up its affordable computing power business. Thus, the project was extended to product-service system design, which specified a complete overview of service and product touchpoints.

Design phase

The design phase focused on the development of one of the product touchpoints; i.e., the heater in which the servers that generate computing power and heat consumers' houses would be placed. *npk design* used drawings, and 2D and 3D visualizations to visualize the appearance of the heater. To provide insight into what the heater would look like in consumers' houses, they also created visualizations showing the heater in its real environment (e.g., the living room). In this phase, Nerdalize provided feedback on the visualizations that the designers of *npk design* created to ensure that the outcome was in line with their needs. *npk design* also played a role in the engineering of the product (e.g., by investigating the cooling apparatus component of the heater), while software development was handled by Nerdalize (e.g., the calculations concerning the servers' computing power). The design phase ended with prototyping and testing of the heater.

Strategy phase

In the strategy phase, *npk design* went through a process of product-service system design together with Nerdalize, which involved performing an extensive overview of product and service touchpoints. This process was important to set up the entire Nerdalize enterprise coherently, instead of just focusing on one of the touchpoints; i.e., the heater. The strategy phase started with ethnographic user research, carried out in tandem with Nerdalize. Nerdalize was also closely involved in the iterations that followed. The insights from the ethnographic user research provided input for a business-modelling workshop, in which *npk* designers stepped back and let Nerdalize take the lead, resulting in a stakeholder value map. In the strategy phase, designers from *npk design* and Nerdalize stakeholders also jointly created a customer journey and a service blueprint. All insights from this phase were summarized in a document, including the service guidelines for all of Nerdalize's service (e.g., call centre, installer) and product (e.g., heater, app, website) touchpoints.

Realization phase
npk design helped Nerdalize to select
the appropriate producer, provided
the producer with information, kept
Nerdalize updated about the process of
production, and ensured that the heaters
were produced according to pre-existing
standards of quality. When the first
series of heaters was produced, *npk
design* assisted Nerdalize in installing the
heaters for the pilot.

After the project
Nerdalize continued improving the
proposition of their product-service
system. *npk design* is involved in the
improvement of this proposition and in
the design of other touchpoints.

The *Bike Accessory project* (Box 4.1) resulted in outcomes that can be described as incremental innovation. In this project, the practices of *making the process accountable* and *tangible* – and the related abilities of *overseeing the process* and *steering the process forward* – were of particular relevance. These practices ensured that SKS Germany (the client) was kept informed and that a 'smooth' process was being followed. The designers' abilities to *adjust the process iteratively* and to *connect* enabled them to steer and manage the project from one originally aimed at the development of style guides to one focused more broadly on portfolio management, and to establish a more long-term relationship with SKS Germany.

The practice of *bringing the solution of the process to life* was particularly of relevance at the end of the design phase, when the outcome crystallized. The designers created multiple visualizations of interim outcomes and created a number of personas. SKS Germany became *acclimated to the ways of working of the designers* through three workshops held during the strategy phase, in which the designers actively engaged SKS Germany team members in the design activities.

In contrast to the Bike Accessory project, the outcomes of the *Cloud Heater project* (Box 4.2) can be described as radically new. For this project, the practices of *making the process accountable and tangible* were used to help the client 'get a grip' on the process, and to devise 'the right way' to go. The designers tried to make the process accountable and tangible mainly by codifying information in written form (e.g., project proposals, contracts, meeting reports, project reports, memos) and via extensive explanations of the process and demonstrations of the tools and techniques it would involve (e.g., stakeholder mapping, customer journey mapping, service blueprinting, etc.).

The practices of *synchronizing the designers' and organizations' processes* and *creating ownership for the process* and related abilities allowed *npk design* to involve Nerdalize in shaping the process. For example, the designers shared information on a continuous basis, iteratively, and on the basis of joint decision-making, the design was adjusted in terms of the products and services to be offered, which led to changes in project planning.

In the Cloud Heater project, it was important to *bring potential solution spaces of the process to life* right from the start, to gauge sentiments and co-create solutions. In particular, the story that the designers created between the service and the product touchpoints was very important. *Acclimating the organization* was important as well, because the project designs involved methods and practices that the organization was not used to. As noted by an involved *npk* designer: 'We make jumps that are different. So I have to detach them from their old way of working, we have to hop around, to figure out the right way to do it'. Interim outcomes were iterated together with the organization. The designers' ability to *create engagement* throughout the process made Nerdalize feel like it was part of the team, and allowed it to participate fully in the design activities ('I really feel that we've created [the results] together! (...) I am really proud of something that we made as a team').

4.5

Conclusion

The main objective of this chapter was to identify relevant design practices and abilities for creating process understanding. To do so, we conducted a case study of *npk design*, and two innovation projects that were conducted by this design consultancy.

The chapter described the six practices (see Table 4.1) and six abilities (see Table 4.2) designers need to create process understanding. Furthermore, we specified how the design practices and abilities are related (see Table 4.2). Concrete examples demonstrated how these practices and abilities were enacted in practice. As shown in Figure 4.1, it is particularly important in the strategy and design phases to create process understanding, and

less so in the realization phase. Our research suggests that creating process understanding by means of our six identified practices and abilities is of particular importance for projects that result in radically novel outcomes. However, when projects have more incremental outcomes, our identified practices and abilities are helpful too, in particular the practices of making the *process accountable* and *making the process tangible,* and the abilities to *oversee the process* and *steer the process forward.*

Overall, strategic designers who create process understanding make uncertain strategic challenges surmountable and help organizations to recognise, respect and invest in the creative design process.

About the authors

KASIA TABEAU was born in 1985 in Warsaw, Poland. She studied Industrial Design Engineering (BSc and MSc) at Delft University of Technology (The Netherlands). After graduating in 2011 (cum laude), she became a PhD researcher in Strategic Design at the same university, pursuing her research career in the Product Innovation Management department. Her PhD research focuses on how designers can play a strategic role in innovation projects by more effectively collaborating with managers. Apart from strategic design, Kasia's research interests include design management, design thinking, service design and user-centred design. Kasia has presented her research at international conferences in marketing, management and innovation, including the EIASM International Product Development Management Conference, the Continuous Innovation Network Conference and the European Marketing Academy Conference. Her research was part of the Creative Industry Scientific Program (CRISP) focusing on stimulating the continuing growth of the Dutch Design Sector and Creative Industries. The CRISP program was sponsored by the Dutch Ministry of Education, Culture, and Science. Kasia is currently an Assistant Professor at Erasmus University Rotterdam.

GERDA GEMSER received her PhD in Management at the Rotterdam School of Management (Erasmus University Rotterdam). Gerda does research on design and innovation management in the creative industries. She has been a visiting scholar at leading research universities, including The Wharton School, the University of Pennsylvania (US) and the Sauder School of Business, University of British Columbia (Canada). Over the last 15 years, she has held assistant and associate professorships at different Dutch universities, including Erasmus University and Delft University of Technology (Faculty of Industrial Design Engineering). She has collaborated with Dutch government, Dutch professional design associations, and Dutch industry on different large-scale research projects to examine the role of design in the corporate world. Currently she is one of five international Professors of Design appointed by RMIT University to further strengthen the university's leadership and expansion of design research. Gerda has published in leading management and design journals including, for example, Organization Science, Organization Studies, Journal of Management, Long Range Planning, Journal of Product Innovation Management, Design Studies, and International Journal of Design. She is part of the editorial board of Journal of Product Innovation Management and Journal of Design, Business & Society.

JOS OBERDORF has over 30 years' experience as a designer of dozens of products, diverse in character, for companies both small and large. After successfully completing his industrial design studies at the Delft University of Technology and his subsequent AIVE study in Eindhoven (nowadays the Design Academy), Jos began as a designer at Philips Design in 1987. After two years, he switched to *npk design*, a recognized Dutch design consultancy (established in 1985) that manages the entire process from strategy and ideation to engineering, prototyping and production support. Jos has been a managing partner of *npk design* since 1998, responsible for daily operations management, design team direction, design strategy formulation(s), and overseeing *npk*'s external communications. Jos has been part-time Professor of Product Architecture Design at Delft University of Technology (Faculty of Industrial Design Engineering) since 2015. Jos is also a founding partner of Yard9, a group of professional Dutch service providers focusing on the Turkish market; and of Denkstof, a multidisciplinary group of architecture-related companies focusing on innovation in building. Together with Wolfram Peters, he was awarded Amsterdam Fund for the Arts' prestigious *Kho Liang Ie* award for the design of Wila Leuchten GmbH in 1997. This is one of the most important personal design awards in the Netherlands.

References

Calabretta, G., Gemser, G., 2015. Integrating Design into the Fuzzy Front End of the Innovation Process, PDMA's Essentials 2: Design and Design Thinking. John Wiley and Sons, New York.

Duck, K., 2012. Executing Strategy: What Designers Can Teach Project Managers. Design Management Review 23, 28-36.

Golsby-Smith, T., 2007. The Second Road of Thought: How Design Offers Strategy a New Toolkit. Journal of Business Strategy 28, 22-29.

Michlewski, K., 2008. Uncovering Design Attitude: Inside the Culture of Designers. Organization Studies 29, 373-392.

PART III

Orchestrating a strategic design project

MARZIA ARICÒ
Livework

MELVIN BRAND FLU
Livework

Aligning organizations through Customer Stories

5.1

Introduction

The business world is slowly waking up to the incredible potential design has to achieve impact for customers and organizations. Organizations are realizing that traditional ways of solving business challenges – process improvements, automation – do not lead to tangible benefits beyond a certain point. Design disciplines such as strategic design and service design, as well as methods like co-creation and customer journey mapping, offer alternative solutions that question the assumptions that subtend a problem, reframe the challenge and ultimately point towards unexpected solutions.

Yet this shiny façade of growing possibilities for design practice hides a much darker, more chaotic situation. Designers are trained to operate at the edge of business development, and thus many of them lack a profound understanding of how organizations operate day to day. Designers are often trained to explore and make sense of what organizations say they need and expect – they may sometimes be trained to perceive what is technically feasible, but very often have a limited understanding of what creates business value, and most importantly, how to navigate the organizational maze of politics, policies, processes, procedures and practices. The deficiency of their understanding becomes strikingly apparent during the design of new services, that, in order to be delivered, necessarily depend upon the coordination of a number of different departments, and often require organizations to effect changes to the operations that structure these domains. Failing to take into consideration existing organizational structure during the design stage will certainly mean failure at the service implementation phase.

Over our last 16 years at Livework, we have experienced all of this first hand. Livework is one of the first service design agencies in the world. Since very early in its inception, agency founders Lavrans Løvlie and Ben Reason have been shaping the discipline and practice of what is

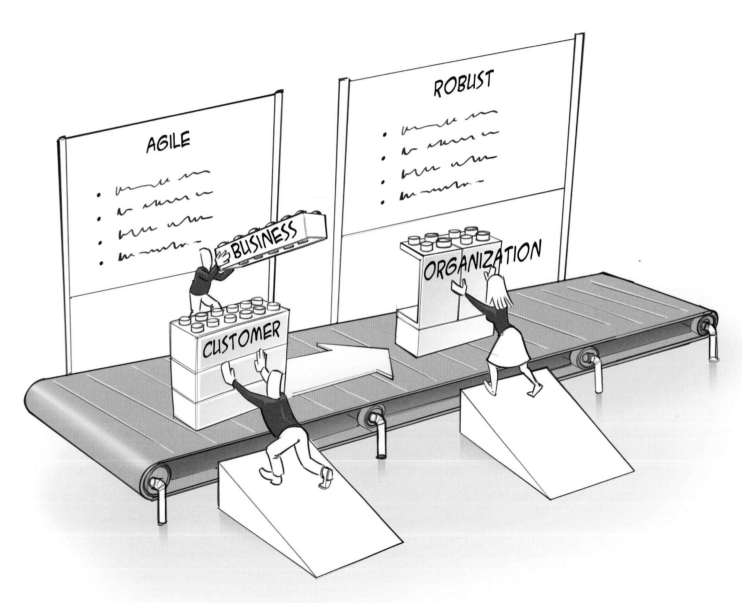

today called 'Service Design' from the ground up. In 2012, new partner Melvin Brand Flu joined the venture. Melvin is not a designer, but a professional with a business consulting background. Joining together a business perspective with a designerly one has enabled Livework to address organizational development that is increasingly strategic in nature, and served to further professionalise their inter-organizational relationships.

This chapter is the result of a deep reflection on the journey made so far. It contains some of Livework's most central insights, with the conviction that these will be useful and relevant for strategic designers struggling to be effective in the context of their client organizations.

Three principles actively drive our work. These are *Nail the Customer Story*, *Translate the Story Across Different Business Units*, and *Design for Multispeed Impact* (Figure 5.1). The three principles together seek to ensure that any strategic design outcome we produce is aligned with the client, the client's business and the client organization. Therefore, by using these three principles in practice, our designers are able to obtain and utilize a profound understanding of a given context – the combination of an organization's needs, wants and expectations, plus their business drivers and capabilities. Articulating this understanding can enable design professionals to clearly perceive the organizational context in which they are operating, and will ultimately present

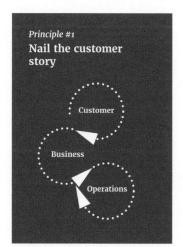
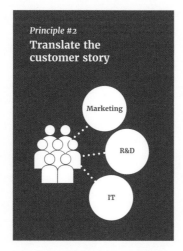
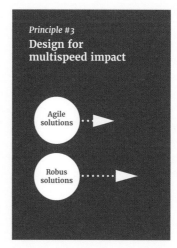

Figure 5.1: Three principles for aligning the organization

them with a fundamental strategic choice – to design within the given boundaries of the context, or change the context. The business and the organization represent an important context for designers to understand and operate within. The 'business context' refers to financial and operational performance, but also to things like market share and competitive advantage (on the topic of understanding the business context see also Chapter 7). The 'organizational context' involves not only people, processes and systems, but also hierarchies and internal politics. A deeper understanding of this environment gives the designer the opportunity to work effectively within it. In some situations, however, it is important for designers to break away – to shatter the context – in order to achieve success and

be effective. We call the first case *acting within*, and the latter *changing the context*. When acting within the context, designers strategically choose to operate within a given set of boundaries. They tailor the design to suit systems already in place, or to the organization's existing knowledge, policies or processes. They build on existing procedures, and produce agile solutions resulting from a combination of the designer's vision and existing organizational capabilities. When changing the context, designers achieve a more thorough understanding of the business and organization, which enables them to strategize solutions for long-term change that will have a more encompassing impact on the organization itself. Because such robust solutions lead the organization on a journey toward profound transformation, they require a strong

commitment from the organization in order to succeed.

Regardless of the approach the strategic designer chooses – acting within or changing a given context – the three principles shared in this chapter will serve to establish the relevance of strategic design among public and private sector organizations that are coming to understand the importance of innovation. This chapter will present and illustrate these three principles through three short case studies. Each of the cases is an authentic solution developed by Livework together with its client organizations. Moreover, although in our arguments we refer to the broader strategic design implications, our experience and analysis mainly concerns the practice of service design.

5.2

Principle #1: Nail the customer story

Typically, organizations structure their teams, systems, processes and policies in a way that fosters a silo mentality. As a result, different departments end up pulling in different directions in order to fulfil different priorities. The user or customer, however, can provide the organization with a more unified view of the organization, by focusing and valuing only an organization's offering and its touchpoints. Customer narratives flatten silos, and make departmental differences irrelevant. Therefore, a simple customer story is the most effective tool you have as a designer to overcome silo thinking and align divergent organizational stakeholders with the project at hand.

In order to clarify this fundamental principle, let's take an example from the telecommunications sector. A customer of a telecom provider based in Germany has an issue with her mobile subscription. The bill turned out to be higher than she had expected. She calls customer service, and somebody from the call centre informs her that the bill is correct, her expectations were wrong, and that she didn't read the contract through. Upset by the response, the customer visits one of the branches, and asks the salesperson to terminate her subscription. The sales assistant has no knowledge of the conversation the customer had on the phone, and hence has no knowledge of the state of agitation the customer is already in. The sales assistant acknowledges that the subscription sold to her only six months before in a 'partner store' is unsuited to her needs, and suggests a new package with a discount. The customer decides to take the new offer and stay with the telecom provider, but the overall experience means that she will likely defect to another provider as soon as she can get out of the contract.

Let's analyse what really happened in this story. The customer sees the telecom provider as one company – the call centre, the branch and partner store are simply perceived as different manifestations of the company. The employee working at the outsourced call centre is measured on the basis of call handling time and overall NPS (Net Promoter Score). The call centre operator has access to the call centre customer contact system, and uses a pre-written script to interact with the customer. The employee working at the branch, on the other hand, is measured in terms of sales volume and has access to a different branch of the customer contract system. The partner store has limited access to a customer's contact history, and the staff is incentivized through new contracts sold. The customer management systems do not communicate enough, so the employees have a fragmented view of the customer story. They are all trying to achieve individual goals, fulfilling their respective priorities of fast call resolution and sales, ignoring what the customer really needs. The employees have only a very narrow view of the customer experience, and the services their organization provides. The customer is the only one that sees the organization as one unified entity, rather than a composite of different departments.

Customers have stories about what they are trying to do with their lives; about their work and leisure or about the people they love. These stories are sometimes good, others are bad – the fluctuations between these highs and lows are our constant experience in life. Customers' life experiences are impacted by the services they use – public transport, inpatient hospital care, mobile phone and data connectivity and so on. People have lives – services are simply extensions that enhance these life experiences. Customer stories therefore cut through business jargon and customer experience/UX/Service Design jargon, which enables designers to get back to real people, and devise measures that add real value to their lives. A customer story is usually a short, simple sentence that expresses the core of what the designer wants to aim for. The process of simplifying the story is not an easy task, and requires a deep understanding of people. Crafting the story requires the designer to go through many iterations and tests to ensure the story is general enough for a diverse group of organizational stakeholders to relate to, but also focused enough to be actionable. Experience makes the process easier over time, enabling the designer to develop the intuition required to build a good story. Each organization can have multiple customer stories whose relevance depends on a given project focus. In the case of the telecom provider, our customer story became 'Customers want an accurate and understandable bill that meets their expectations'. Having such a brief and concise sentence enabled us to meet two objectives: it captured the core of what adds value for the customer in a manner understandable to any stakeholder, and it tells the story of the improved service we want the organization to provide. When well formulated, the customer story becomes a powerful tool used to ensure buy-in across different organizational units – any unit can relate to it. In our example, what the story describes is a service provider getting the basics right.

The customer story is usually connected to a specific period in the customer lifecycle. A customer lifecycle as explained by Reason et al. is a framework that 'describes the phases and stages customers move through during their relationship with a sector' (2016, p. 168). The lifecycle runs through the phases before the customer actually buys or joins, continues through the purchase, early setup and daily use, eventually covering the process of reconsidering and leaving. The customer lifecycle changes from sector to sector, but is always built around a specific structure which includes a 'before', a 'beginning', a 'during' and an 'after'. Making the customer story adhere to a specific lifecycle stage means that, depending on the project and the designer's objective, there will certainly be a few customer stories – one per lifecycle phase under analysis.

Each customer story will eventually be visualized as a customer journey. Customer journeys are used to describe specific experiences from a customer's perspective, and home in on the details of the customer experience – the tasks they need to perform, and the interactions they have during their service journey. They provide increased granularity in the designer's understanding of a specific aspect – like 'onboarding', for example – of the overall customer experience.

Using the customer story and related journey will have two consequences: business units will clearly see how the customer experiences the organization – as one unified entity, rather than in terms of their individual silos – and they will also immediately understand their specific role in delivering that experience. The customer story can be used *as is* – what customers are currently experiencing with a service – to critically examine the status quo, or describe *what is to be* – what designers would like customers to experience in the future – to strategize roles and responsibilities in relation to the design of a brand new experience.

CASE STUDY: energy provider, UK.

A British energy provider has invested an extensive period of time in nailing the right customer story. They called upon Livework to show them how to use the customer story to align the company's channels, functions, processes and metrics in a simple manner. The goal was to align different business units by providing a holistic picture of the functional activities that support the customer story, the business processes that are impacted and specific key performance indicators (KPIs). This effort has enabled the energy provider to broadcast a shared understanding of the envisioned customer experience across different business units, and further the development of the project with a clear understanding of the real, organizational impact that new vision would have. In this case, the customer lifecycle covered the following stages: 'shop' (customer evaluates different options and decides on one), 'join' (customer buys from the energy provider), 'use & help' (customer gets into regular use and seeks support when needed), 'change' (customer's circumstances change requiring a change in the subscription) and 'departure' (customer defects).

We will analyse the use & help stage in this brief example. The customer story is, 'Our customers only want to pay for the energy they have consumed'. The journey for this story is developed around four stages (Figure 5.2): 'prompting' (the customer receives a notification asking for meter reading), 'give reading' (the customer provides the reading), 'receive bill' and 'understand bill'. Each stage is subsequently described in greater detail according to a number of specifications, such as customer needs and customer engagement.

The customer story and its specifications enable us to: 1) visually grasp the customer story, 2) understand where that story sits within the overall customer experience, 3) understand what the customer's needs are at that moment, 4) clarify the outcome we want to achieve, 5) clarify the experience we want to foster, and 5) list the touchpoints we will use to make it happen.

Designers might perceive the customer story as level zero of their analysis.

Prompting   **Give reading**   **Receive bill**   **Understand bill**   **Understand bill**
(when contacting)

Figure 5.2: A visualization depicting the 'use & help' section of the energy customer journey

In order to use it effectively it must be aligned with the *business* story, to demonstrate how it interacts with the organization. Our customer story for the use & help phase therefore evolved into 'Our customers want to only pay for the energy they have consumed, and our business processes do not make that as easy as it should be. We generate 35% of our bills according to estimated readings, which creates unnecessary costs of £200 million annually'. This becomes level 1 of our analysis. It brings together customer desires and expectations with what the company eventually delivers. As per the customer story, the business story is also detailed across the different stages of the lifecycle. Level 2 of our analysis aligns the customer and business stories with the operational story. This third level often uncovers the source of some customers' pain points and the business failures presented in the first two stories.

Table 5.1: Example of customer, business and organizational story alignment

	Description	Specifications	Specification Example
Customer Activity	Understand bill	–	
Customer Story	Bills & statements are difficult for customers to understand	• Customer Needs • Customer Outcome • Customer Experience • Customer Engagement (key touchpoints)	Customer Need: 'I need my bill to be easy to understand. Why has my bill been estimated?'
Business Story	Customers not understanding bills results in contact	• Growth • Retention • Complaints • Contact • Brand • Compliance	Contact: Bills contain information that customers find confusing: 45% of calls at call centre are bill-related
Operational Story	Only 65% of bills are generated after actual meter readings	• People • Processes • Technology • Information • Policy	People: Our people produce many bills that are unscheduled

Table 5.1 shows an example of the three high-level stories aligned in relation to the customer journey stage 'understand bill'. The table also lists all the detailing parameters applied to each story. This approach enabled the design team to truly understand the context, and ascertain the most effective direction to take. Our service design efforts eventually managed to align the business and organization stories to the customer story, enabling the organization to deliver what customers really wanted in a way that made business sense and could be delivered using existing organizational capabilities. This is the moment when strategic design fulfils its potential.

5.3

Principle #2: Translate the story across different business units

Strategic design has an impact on the roles and activities of staff across the entire organization. For most people change is a threat, therefore early-stage involvement of staff is fundamental to be able to align the organization with a novel design. The involvement of employees from different levels in the organizational hierarchy is extremely valuable, and often guarantees ownership of change (on the topic of ownership also see Chapter 2 and Chapter 3). Designers are particularly good at engaging and exciting crowds. Everyone likes to take a day off from his or her routine to participate in a well-designed creative workshop. That's the easy part. The most complicated task is to cement engagement (see also Chapter 2) and long-term commitment (see also Chapter 8), maintain momentum and incorporate the new design into the everyday working lives of different people in different positions across the organization. Engagement is not simply informing and requiring change, but involving employees actively in the process of change, by focusing on their insights, ideas and feedback.

In order to engage the wider organization, being able to tell the right story to the right person becomes fundamental in the process. Knowing what staff members in different departments care about and building on that becomes a huge advantage for strategic designers who seek to achieve long-term organizational commitment, buy-in and alignment. A strategic designer needs to understand the general goal of each business unit and the way employees' work is measured, and therefore rewarded. That information becomes key to designing the right story for each business unit – one that will convince people, excite them, engage them and eventually align them. The use of customized stories will facilitate a designer's success in the long term.

CASE STUDY: telecom + banking, Russia

A Russian joint venture between a telecommunications provider and a bank asked Livework to design the customer experience around a brand new product they were developing. The product was a package combining a mobile subscription (including mobile phone) and a credit line (including a credit card). Russia is a cash-driven country where people are extremely sceptical about the very concept of credit lines, and where distrust for banks is very high. In order to facilitate the acceptance of credit cards, the client decided to develop a new product available with a mobile subscription. Their goal is a high volume of credit line activation and use. Their objective is therefore a long-term one – the product is extremely innovative in that specific market, so the project is highly strategic for the company.

The complexity of the service would reach every aspect of the business and require a level of collaboration between departments that exceeded normal operations. Senior management knew that following a traditional product development route would result in the launch of an immature service that was not properly supported by the organization. Given the market and reputational risk involved, we developed a customer story to guide the development of the service and prepare the organization to launch it successfully. The core of the customer story rested on three main pillars: enabling people to learn about the benefits of the service when it seemed important to them, getting customers to try it with an x dollar incentive, no strings attached – even hidden ones, and ultimately building trust over time so that people would increasingly start using it. The customer story became 'I was offered this great service, which did not only lower my purchase by x dollars, it actually automatically insured my purchase. The more I use the service or get others to join, the more benefits come my way. Since this sounds too good to be true, I'll start by taking the initial offer and see what happens...'

The business case for this service requires a high adoption rate and increasing usage over the first two years. The internal versions of the story therefore focused on the period that would follow the launch of the service. Given the complexity and the breadth of the project, multiple business units had to be involved. Therefore, different stories were designed to excite and engage diverse business units, with the ultimate goal of aligning them towards the same vision. Their role in the delivery of this brand new service also meant that there would be changes to the way their performance was measured. Table 5.2 provides a detailed

Table 5.2: Translating the customer story across different business units

Functions	General Unit Objectives	General Unit Measurement	Internal Story for the Service	Effect of the Story
Sales	To sell more via direct and indirect channels. Upselling, cross selling, contract renewals or continuation.	Current: Number of sales, or value of sales. To be introduced: Volume and value of people using the credit card. Not just activation but those brought on board long-term.	The service is completely new for customers. They will need help using it the first time, and clear direction regarding why they should use the service more frequently. The sale is no longer finalised when you close a contract.	The sales unit collaborates with other departments to help incentivize use of the service, and does not just sell the initial service.
Marketing	Organize campaigns, activities and events to reach general audiences or specific customer groups.	Current: Level of adoption, customer feedback, volume of new customers acquired. To be introduced: Level of adoption over two years. Word of mouth.	Customers need to be made aware of the service as being part of a mobile purchase. They need to understand the benefits of using the service frequently. It's not just about attracting but fostering future service use.	The marketing team designs campaigns that run for over 2 years, from the moment the customers signs up for the service.
Operations	Keep the business running and deal with issues that have an effect on operations.	Current: Time performance, number of incidents/defects, quality standards. To be introduced: Conversion to the next tier of usage. Frequency of service use. Any customer interaction should be skewed towards educating them.	Any customer interaction should be skewed towards educating them. Every customer contact should be focused on educating and incentivizing frequent use. Therefore an excellent service experience becomes necessary.	Customer support activities are redesigned from resolving an incident to engaging the customer in a conversation in order to make them feel comfortable enough to use the service more.
IT	Implement, support and improve IT systems, which run and support the business.	Current: Incidents and defects recorded, speed and accuracy of transactions, financial and operational performance. To be introduced: Provide cross-channel IT service.	Make it simple for the customer. Customers should feel comfortable using the service. We need to know who is using the service, how, and which incentive is the most appropriate in any given situation.	The data is pushed to all relevant internal departments as well as third parties who interact with customers. This enables the organization to be more proactive in approaching customers.
HR	Attract, retain and develop people in the business.	Current: Staff retention, satisfaction and (certified) skill levels. To be introduced: Customer satisfaction.	The service requires a high degree of trust, and therefore sales and support staff need to inform and educate the customer at the same time.	Special training of sales and support staff in how to inform customers and educate them without pushing them too hard.

explanation of each business unit, their general goal, the way they were measured at the time the project began, and the new measures to be introduced as per service implementation, a sample story used to engage them and a description of the effect the story was intended to produce. The content contained in the table was shaped by the Livework team using our knowledge of the sector combined with an in-depth analysis of the client's specific context and organizational architecture.

This case is another example of *acting within.* The design team heavily invested in gaining a deep understanding of the client's business and organizational context, to maximise their ability to work within it.

5.4

Principle #3: Design for multispeed impact

As strategic designers, we are used to adopting the human perspective. Understanding humans and designing something that can perfectly fit their needs, desires and expectations is at the core of everything we do. More often rather than not however, organizations are simply not prepared to deliver on the design because it cannot readily implement the required organizational changes that support the design. There can be multiple reasons behind this; however, this situation is usually related to the people, systems, processes, procedures or policies already in place. Therefore, the designed strategy should reflect the readiness of the organization to embrace the proposed change.

Strategic design outcomes should be multispeed and enable alignment over time. Particularly, designers should envision both agile (short-term) and robust (long-term) solutions. Agile solutions are quick to deliver and easy to implement. Focusing on some of the easier solutions first sometimes has the effect of making some of the harder issues more manageable, and at times even makes them disappear. Robust solutions are conversely long-term investments requiring more time, resources and planning to implement. A way to strategize around a multispeed approach is to start from customers' needs, which can in fact be broken down into three areas: needs for *information*, *interactions*, and *transactions* (Reason et al., 2016). The analysis of each, in the context of the organization and its specific industry, enables designers to move at different speeds for different needs.

The need for information is the need to receive complete and easy to understand information in relation to a product or a service – usually the easiest change to tackle and implement. Changes at an

Figure 5.3: Designing multispeed solutions

informational level generally modify the organization's policies and processes, to enable fast, short-term, agile solutions. Interactions are moments of exchange between customers and the organization. They can happen via people – the staff at a branch or the employees at the call centre for example, via digital tools like a company's app or website or via physical products. Changing an interaction is a bit more complicated than changing the typology of information delivered, as often it requires training people to deliver the new interaction, and also changing some of the practices and processes in place. Changes in interactions will therefore require medium-term planning and design.

Lastly we have the need for transaction, which is the instance of buying or selling something. Changes to the transaction level are extremely difficult, and at times appear threatening to organizations, as they often end up affecting IT legacy systems plus the people, policies, processes and procedures involved. Changes at this level are time consuming and expensive to achieve, requiring a robust vision and a detailed long-term plan.

The movement between addressing informational, interactional or transactional needs enables strategic designers to provide multispeed solutions that are more manageable and realistic for organizations to realise.

CASE STUDY: General Insurance, Norway

A general insurance company in Norway involved Livework to support their goal to become one of the most customer-centric organizations in the country. Moving towards customer centricity felt to our client like a wholesale change at an organizational level, as such a profound transformation would reach every single organizational domain – meaning people, processes, procedures, policies and of course technology. That was too much to handle at once. Therefore the company needed multispeed solutions, including some agile solutions that could bring immediate impact and create excitement and momentum among employees, while building some more robust long-term changes. Our design team let the

customer story drive the process, as per Principle 1, while mapping areas of high and low performance against customer needs. The needs were then broken down into information, interactions and transactions, enabling the company to develop a feasible plan to move everything forward.

One of the first things we did was to create fast and agile solutions that could create momentum at the information level. The initial focus was therefore on contracts, in terms of language used and length. Those contracts were indeed perceived by customers to be overly complicated and too long, and thus simpler contracts were one of the

key customer needs. The team worked to design a contract that was shorter in terms of pages and simpler to understand. Many prototypes were developed and tested with customers to get the language and the length right. A number of people across the organization were involved to ensure that the new design both respected existing organizational contract policies, and could be implemented at scale.

After the initial focus on information, the organization seemed ready for some more complex work at the interaction level. Our focus became the interaction between customers and employees at the call centre. Similar to most call centres around the world, our client's call centre employees had been provided with a script intended to guide their interactions with customers. The first thing that the script required the employee to ask for was the policy number. While interviewing call centre employees, it became apparent that some of the staff opted not to stick to the script, and instead asked a few very simple initial questions, 'How are you? Is everything OK with you and your family?' Those simple questions gave customers the chance to offload the anxiety they had accumulated because of the accident they wanted to claim, and as a result the claim was much more expeditiously resolved. With this insight, our team started working together to empower call centre staff to do their job in a way that was more effective and suited to their role in the interaction. The script was replaced with a set of principles and a set of goals staff were told to keep in mind when dealing with a customer on the phone. Doing so required extensive work on policies and processes already in place, and also required staff at the call centre to get further training to learn how to implement the new practices. This was certainly a more complex endeavour than merely changing the script, but our designs resulted in shorter resolution times and higher ratings on customer satisfaction.

These are two very brief examples of the kind of projects that the organization invested in. Their overall journey towards customer centricity lasted seven years, and in some respects is still ongoing. The multispeed approach driven by customer story and needs has enabled the organization to achieve results consistently and successfully over time, while helping the design team to remain focused and realistic in terms of managing expectations, providing solutions and setting goals. This last case is an example of changing the context. Using a broader, more inclusive view of their organizational context during the design of multispeed solutions enabled the organization to accommodate change little by little, over time, and establish the foundations – in the short term – that would support the more demanding work to be done in the long term.

5.5

Conclusion

Design is becoming of increasingly strategic use to organizations. Nonetheless, to be effective, and establish the credibility needed for businesses to trust them with their strategic choices, designers still have a way to go. A shift towards professionalizing strategic design is now required. By extending the pool of knowledge and expertise related to the ways businesses and organizations operate, strategic design – and designers – will become central to producing innovations that are easier for companies to understand, internalize and implement. The three principles we have introduced in this chapter are the result of our in-depth reflection over more than fifteen years of strategic design practice alongside a number of large organizations operating in more than twenty industries. These principles represent the lessons we have learned through trial and error. We are confident that mastering them will enable strategic designers to build the complementary set of abilities they need to understand the business and the organization, and to design for it. This new set of skills will eventually make strategic designers increasingly credible professionals who understand their context and know how to navigate it best. Eventually the newly-acquired set of abilities, plus the newly-achieved credibility will boost their confidence to truly guide organizations toward the most appropriate solutions for short- and long-term impact. It is going to be a long journey, but it is also a sorely needed one.

About the authors

MARZIA ARICÒ believes in the power of collaborative intelligence and in the potential that exists in the cross-pollination of business and design. Over the past 10 years, alongside more than 100 Global 2000 organizations worldwide, she has been involved in a series of cutting-edge projects intended to embed design thinking into innovation processes. She currently works as Service Design and Strategy Consultant at Livework. She is one of 12 researchers selected worldwide by DESMA, the European Design Management Network, to investigate how design can become a driver for innovation in Europe in the next five years. Marzia is also a PhD fellow at Copenhagen Business School, where she seeks to empirically demonstrate how service design adds value to businesses. She regularly speaks at a number of international conferences and seminars on service design, and she is a visiting professor and speaker at a number of universities worldwide such as Iceland Academy of the Arts, Delft University of Technology, CENTRO, IED and CBS.

MELVIN BRAND FLU is partner of strategy and business design at Livework. His background is a mix of strategy, business, consulting, IT, marketing and finance, which enables him to create lasting impact in complex business environments. For over 25 years, he has been a trusted advisor and trouble-shooter for global brands, start-ups and public sector organizations, where he has delivered and rescued complex projects, often within strict timeframes. He writes books and publishes articles about customer centricity, business impact, service transformation and digital customer relationships. Melvin coaches executives and management teams in how to deliver value to customers, the business and the organization. He leads the Livework Intelligence unit, which performs breakthrough research on consumer and human behaviour that is tested and proven in tandem with his Livework clients.

References

Polaine, A., Løvlie, L., & Reason, B.
(2013) Service Design. From Insight to
Implementation. Rosenfeld Media

Reason, B., Løvlie, L. & Brand Flu, M.
(2016) Service Design for Business. New
Jersey: Wiley

GERDA GEMSER
RMIT University, Melbourne, Australia

BLAIR KUYS
Swinburne University, Melbourne, Australia

OPHER YOM-TOV
Chief Design Officer at ANZ Banking Group

Designing For Feasibility

6.1

Introduction

Innovation is only present when a creative idea is successfully implemented (Amabile, 1988). In other words, innovation does not stop once an opportunity has been identified, it also includes taking the necessary steps to ensure that this opportunity is actually exploited; for example, by developing and introducing a new service to the market. To ensure successful implementation, strategic designers should explicitly take feasibility into account. Feasibility relates to whether an organization actually has – or can acquire in the foreseeable future – the resources and capabilities needed to exploit the identified opportunity.

Let's look at an example. In Australia, the topic of superannuation (retirement funds that can be actively managed by consumers) is not in the forefront of people's minds, especially younger people's minds. A relatively simple solution to highlight the opportunities presented by superannuation, and thus forge a closer relationship with those saving for it, is to provide them with the option to view and manage their retirement funds while doing their online banking. Each time people check their day-to-day transactions online,

they would also be able to view their superannuation balance and have the option to manage those funds as they would a debit account. While the idea is relatively simple and clearly desirable, it has proven challenging to implement – the processes and technologies that would support it are very difficult to reconfigure in such a way that they work together with any degree of reliability. Reconfiguration would require, for example, the integration of multiple 'legacy' systems across many parts of the organization. In other words, a simple idea to cater for a (latent) consumer need requires an incredible effort to be actually implemented (see Figure 6.1).

Explicitly taking feasibility into account when designing requires designers to use a specific approach that combines 'blue sky' thinking and pragmatism. Considering that these are two potentially opposing approaches, their combination may, in practice, present designers with a real challenge. To address the feasibility issue in this chapter, we emphasize the important role of co-creation with a team of domain experts. Although co-creation is often studied in terms of organizations that innovate in close collaboration with end users or consumers (e.g., Gemser and Perks, 2016), in this chapter, we employ the term co-creation to refer to strategic designers who co-create with other domain specialists to ensure that a project is feasible.

There are core questions that strategic designers, and the teams they operate in, should ask themselves in order to assess whether the opportunities they identify are feasible. These can be summarized as follows:

1. What resources and capabilities does the organization need to translate the identified opportunity into actual products and services?
2. Does the organization have those resources and capabilities, or is investment needed to 'stretch' available resources and capabilities? Do investments need to be made to acquire new resources and capabilities?
3. If investments need to be made to extend or bring in new resources and capabilities, will the organization have the financial means to do so?

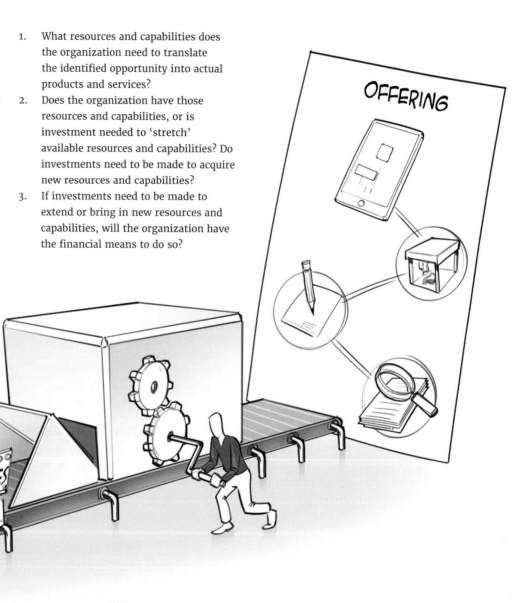

With the term 'resource', we mean an input into an organization's production process. A resource can be *tangible*, and thus be seen or quantified (such as, for example, available financial funds, manufacturing machines, available distribution channels or human resources). A resource can also be *intangible*, and thus more difficult to measure (such as an organization's reputation or brand identity). A 'capability', on the other hand, refers to an organization's ability to utilise its resources in a successful way. Superior innovation management, superior portfolio management, excellent customer service and marketing excellence are all examples of capabilities that help to create competitive advantage. Capabilities are developed over time, while resources can be relatively easily bought or imitated. While an organization with money could buy the technology and the physical plant and equipment needed to manufacture smart phones, it would be much harder to transform those resources into the capability to innovate as successfully as, say, Apple does. In the second question listed above, we ask whether resources or capabilities need to be 'stretched', by which we

Figure 6.1: A simple idea drowns in complexity

mean that existing resources and capabilities may have to be adapted or adjusted. If the answer to the second question is 'yes' – that is, there is a need to stretch existing resources and capabilities and/or acquire new ones – then this implies there are likely to be risks. Considering the risk-averse nature of most organizations, the likelihood of implementing this kind of project becomes less certain. Implementation becomes even less likely, at least in the short term, if the organization lacks the financial means to stretch or bring in

the resources and capabilities needed to exploit the opportunity (see question 3). However, if the designer strongly believes that the opportunity identified will bring the organization lucrative rewards, it is his or her responsibility to create a very compelling argument for it. A designer can do this by creating a prototype of the future state, and validate the prototype by testing it with users and staff. If that prototype is also accompanied by a strong business model and implementation plan, then the company has a clearer sense of the payoff versus the investment.

6.2

A framework to assess feasibility

As noted in Chapter 1 (Introduction), designers become strategic when they are able to identify and exploit opportunities that are not only *desirable* but also *viable* and *feasible*. To assess desirability, an extensive analysis of factors and actors external to the organization is needed. To assess viability and feasibility, on the other hand, an in-depth understanding of the organization's internal environment is also required; in turn, this requires an 'audit' of an organization's resources and capabilities, which we will describe in more detail later.

To understand an organization's internal environment, and identify and exploit opportunities that fit with this environment, co-creation with the organization and relevant domain experts is essential. Strategic designers cannot be experts at everything, but they should be specialists of their own domain ('desirability', see Chapter 1: Introduction). However, strategic designers need to invest in understanding and becoming familiar with what other domain experts (e.g., experts in the fields of engineering, marketing or finance) can bring. This will help designers ask the experts the 'right' questions.

Of course, it should ideally be a two-way street – while strategic designers must take the time to understand what other specialists can bring to the project for co-creation to succeed, the other specialists must also become familiar with and relate to the capabilities, skills and working methods of the strategic designers. Indeed, and often, an important task for a strategic designer at the start of a project is to educate others about their skills, methods and tools as these are generally very different from more conventional ones (on the topic of education, see also Chapter 8).

Strategic designers must attempt to minimize project risks by fully considering feasibility *before* proposing new opportunities. However, an audit of an organization's resources and capabilities to assess feasibility should *not* be the starting point of the design process. A strategic designer should not just take an organization's resources and capabilities and then design offerings to suit. She or he needs to use higher-order thinking to devise offerings that actually address an exciting new opportunity so that the organization can innovate and adapt to changing circumstances. Simply designing to suit an organization's current set of resources and capabilities may result in offerings that are too similar to existing ones, and thus may provide little competitive differentiation. In other words, when identifying new opportunities, less emphasis should be given to feasibility. However, when selecting which new opportunities to exploit, feasibility then becomes a high priority.

In Figure 6.2, the *vertical axis* shows the level of aspiration of an identified opportunity, which can fluctuate from low to high. Low aspiration means that the new opportunity will be translated into a concrete form (e.g., product, service) that differs only in an incremental way from competitive offerings and, in general, will provide little competitive advantage. High aspiration, on the other hand, means translation into a concrete form that is radically different from what went before, potentially resulting in sustained competitive advantage. The *horizontal axis* shows the degree to which translation of the new opportunity into a concrete form is feasible. To assess feasibility, we examine whether

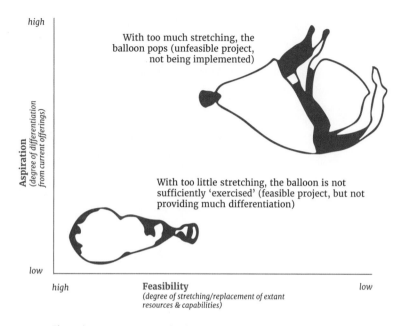

Figure 6.2: Aspiration versus feasibility

translation of the new opportunity requires much stretching or replacement of an organization's existing resources and capabilities. If this is the case, then feasibility is low. The image in the matrix (right-hand corner) represents a balloon being stretched from right to left, which represents the need for adapting existing resources and capabilities. With too much stretching, the balloon pops;

that is, the project becomes unfeasible and will not be implemented. However, with too little stretching, the balloon is insufficiently 'exercised' (see the image at the left-hand bottom of the matrix); that is, the project may be highly feasible, but may not provide much differentiation. Thus, exploitation of the opportunity may not deliver an enduring competitive advantage.

Implementing radically new ideas often seems 'too' risky. In fact, innovation projects fail to be implemented because they appear to ask the organization to stretch their existing capabilities and resources too far. It is the responsibility of strategic designers and their team members to attenuate that sense of risk by demonstrating feasibility. To do so, strategic designers can follow the 'resource/capability-gap' approach (Donlon and Walmer, 2011) represented in Figure 6.3.

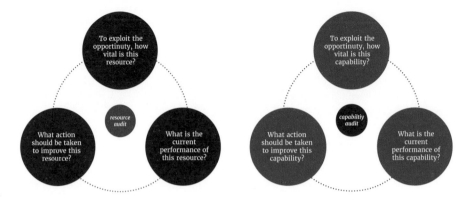

Figure 6.3: Resource/capability gap approach

The 'resource/capability-gap' approach requires, as a first step, identification of the resources and capabilities that are needed to effectively exploit the identified opportunity. It involves asking questions like: *What critical skills or abilities (e.g., being empathetic with the customer) are required from people involved to exploit the opportunity?* and *What are the critical processes (e.g., handling customer complaints) and technology requirements (e.g., software applications that support efficient handling of customer complaints) to exploit the opportunity?* Once a systematic inventory of necessary resources and capabilities is complete, the resource/capability gap can be measured, which means an audit

of the organization's existing resources and capabilities must be carried out. This audit not only needs to identify whether the requisite resources and capabilities are actually present in the organization, but must also rate the 'performance' or 'quality' of those resources and capabilities. An organization might have machines to manufacture plastic buckets, for example, but if those machines are out-dated, the quality of the machines as a resource is low. To be able to assess the resource gap, the design team may need to involve others in the organization and/

or may need to spend a lot of time on the 'shop floor'.

Once the gap has been identified, the final step is to devise initiatives to acquire or improve needed resources and capabilities that are lacking or that score low on performance. For example, successful exploitation of a new opportunity in the field of retail banking may require superior customer service. However, front-desk staff may lack the skill to 'sense' customer needs and wishes. The design team could then propose to train

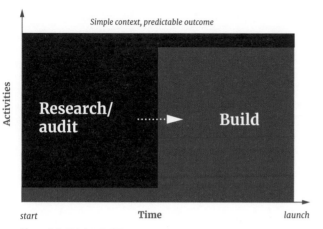

Figure 6.4: Think to build

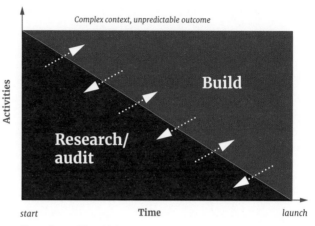

Figure 6.5: Build to think

the staff in human-centric design tools and methods to enhance their empathic skills.

Improving extant resources and capabilities does not necessarily mean building up internal resources. Another effective route – particularly if the organization is lacking in financial means – is to collaborate with external partners. As described in Case Study 1, exploiting a new opportunity may require that an organization shifts away from serving the business-to-business market and moves toward the business-to-consumer market. The organization would probably not have the marketing excellence and

distribution channels to operate in a business-to-consumer market, but it could then collaborate with another organization that possesses the requisite resources and capabilities.

By helping the organization identify resource gaps and showing them how to close those gaps, strategic designers and their teams attenuate the risk the project may present, which increases the chances that the project will actually be implemented. However, as Case Study 2 will show, a resource/capability audit is not just a one-off activity. It is something that needs to be performed continually – especially if the project

involves a radically new idea and a complex context – because it will be hard to specify up front the resources and capabilities that may be needed down the line. 'Audits' for complex projects need to be iterative and continue during the 'building' phase. Designers should then 'build to think' rather than 'think to build'; Figures 6.4 and 6.5 visualize this idea. In relatively simple contexts, with relatively predictable outcomes, a comprehensive, upfront resource/capability audit makes sense (see Case Study 1); in a more complex context with more unpredictable outcomes, the audit needs to be an on-going process (see Case Study 2).

6.3

Case studies

The two case studies presented below demonstrate the ideas we have presented via 'real-world' examples. Our first case study shows how designers helped a company find new markets for their products. While the designers very strategically co-determined the future direction of the company, the context was such that the resource/capability audit could be performed up front. Our second case study relates to a very innovative idea and a very complex context, and so the feasibility audit was an ongoing activity. Teamwork with the relevant feasibility experts was central to each design's success.

Case Study 1: Designing feasible market diversification

This case study looks at an Australian plastics manufacturing company that had been predominantly supplying low-cost parts to the Australian automotive industry. Their product line included hubcaps, sensor caps, bumpers and trim. The company needed to diversify into other markets, otherwise it might have ceased to exist, especially considering that every Australian-based automotive manufacturer had decided to eventually move their manufacturing offshore: Ford in 2016, General Motors (GM) Holden in 2017 and Toyota in 2017 (Australian Government Department of Industry and Science, 2015).

The manufacturing company did not have much experience innovating because it had always benefitted from known quantities and known markets. The company did, however, have vast experience driving efficiencies in its business, as it had always been under constant pressure from the big automotive companies to continually cut costs. Furthermore, many of the company's employees had 20+ years of experience in their respective fields, and were committed to change to preserve their jobs. There was zero resistance to change – the organization just did not know how to go about it.

The company gave the second author and his design team the assignment to develop new products for markets the company was not yet serving. The design team had to work with two major challenges related to feasibility:

1. The new products were to be manufactured using existing in-house capabilities and resources as far as possible, due to resource constraints – the company was in financial 'survival mode'.
2. The product had to be aimed at a market that – while not yet being served by the company – was already well developed, and sought low-cost, mass-produced yet quality-based plastic products.

These constraints obviously restricted design freedom; however, they also helped to calibrate the concepts to ensure that final outcomes could be produced efficiently and effectively. Apart from these practical concerns, the design team also had the challenge of working with a company that was inexperienced in innovating and which had some difficulty thinking outside the box.

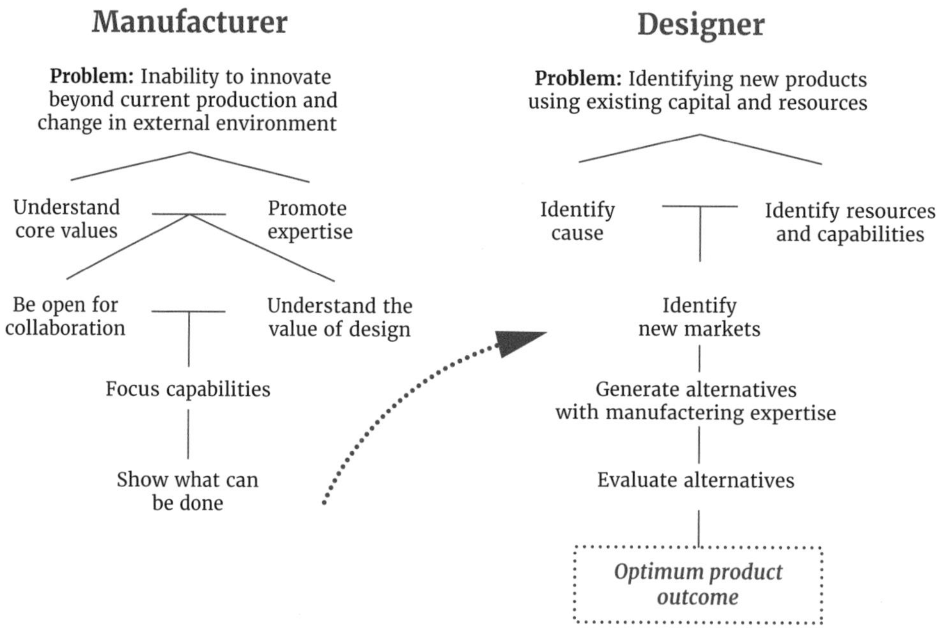

Manufacturer

Problem: Inability to innovate beyond current production and change in external environment

Understand core values — Promote expertise

Be open for collaboration — Understand the value of design

Focus capabilities

Show what can be done

Designer

Problem: Identifying new products using existing capital and resources

Identify cause — Identify resources and capabilities

Identify new markets

Generate alternatives with manufactering expertise

Evaluate alternatives

Optimum product outcome

Figure 6.6: Decision tree for finding new markets.

In Figure 6.6, a tree diagram visually communicates the project's intent.

To fulfil the brief, the design team carried out a resource/capability audit of the company's existing resources and capabilities up front. The designers asked questions including, for example, *What does the company excel in, and what is the company doing less well?* and *What type of resources does the company have, and do these resources have unique, competitive value?* This audit was not easy, as much of the organization's knowledge of their existing capabilities and resources was tacit and thus needed to be codified. The first thing the design team did was to connect with the people on the shop floor – considerable time was spent standing next to machine operators. Many weeks passed before any designing took place, which not only culminated in a more complete understanding of the organization's concrete resources and existing capital equipment, but also in a much deeper understanding of the company culture. Naturally, if ideas are proposed that do not suit the company culture, those involved in their implementation tend to show very little commitment to those ideas. Producing plastic flowers and plants, for example, would probably encounter considerable resistance from a group of automotive engineers!

Once the resource/capability audit was performed, a team of designers and experts from inside the organization generated ideas that aligned with the organization's resources and capabilities; in fact, these experts (engineers and

Figure 6.7: Work closely with the company employees to understand the capabilities and resources you are designing for

machine operators) were involved in every stage of the design process. This gave the experts a sense of ownership, and helped the designers prepare the products' designs and tooling. Another major benefit for such close engagement was that the manufacturing company and its employees were exposed first-hand to design methods and tools, which in turn made it easier for them to embrace design as an organizational capability (on embracing design as an organizational capability, see Chapter 8).

Once concepts were developed, they were evaluated by a multidisciplinary team of designers, engineers and marketers from outside the organization. The unbiased, external evaluation they made of the proposed designs, together with session outcomes, were used to help justify the concepts that were subsequently presented to the organization's management team.

Five new product concepts were presented in total. Figure 6.8 shows one example of a product developed – a small plastic paint bucket that innovates upon those usually sold in your local hardware store. Obviously, a plastic bucket is hardly a revolutionary product advancement, but the innovative features make it more than just another plastic thing.

At the time of writing, the paint bucket mentioned in this case study is going through tooling, and full production will commence towards the end of 2016. The rights to distribute the product have been purchased by a leading cleaning products company with large distribution channels in the major hardware and supermarket chains. Exclusive/sole manufacturing rights remain with the manufacturing company.

PAINT BUCKET

This is a paint bucket that significantly exceeds existing products in the home D.I.Y area.

This bucket would be used to hold paint that is poured from a larger tin (4L, 10L & 15L), allowing users to conveniently move paint and brush to the desired area.

Current products lack the ability to place your paintbrush in the bucket without it falling further into the paint, as well as the standard ergonomic and practicality issues with existing products.

Competitors are yet to find a solution to carrying and then holding your paint whilst working from a ladder.

WIPE DETAIL
Allows the user to wipe the excess paint from brush without causing paint to run down the side of the bucket

OVER MOULDED MAGNET
Allows the user to place their paintbrush against the wall of the bucket when not in use

MOULDED LABEL AREA
Allows for a dynamically shaped label to be incorporated into the bucket

HANDLE LOCATION
Avoids unnecessary tilting and movement of paint within the bucket

FINGER CAVITY
Allows the bucket to be held with one hand without using the handle

Figure 6.8: The final presentation board used to visually represent the product outcome

Case Study 2: Designing iteratively for feasibility, or 'building a foundation while constructing the house'

This second case study relates to AirShr, a new technology venture co-founded by the third author of this chapter.

The start-up seeks to provide a digital service that enables radio listeners to capture, replay and share anything they hear on the radio, including music, ads, talk shows and news. By means of a smartphone app and a small Bluetooth remote device, listeners can capture an entire radio segment with the tap of a button. Within a few seconds, the entire segment is sent to their mobile device, accompanied by images, web links, videos and supporting text. AirShr also provides real-time information to radio broadcasters and advertisers about how audiences are responding to their content – a capability previously

unheard of in the radio industry.

The start-up idea emerged from an experience co-founder Phil Hayes-St Clair had while driving. He heard a radio commercial for a music concert and was struggling to capture the details in the car. After unsuccessfully searching for a solution to this problem, he approached the third author and another friend with the digital service idea.

While scoping this business concept, the co-founders asked themselves three initial questions: (1) *Do people want to remember what they hear on the radio (desirability)?* (2) *How might this proposition create value (viability)?* and (3) *How can we enable the seamless capture and review of any item broadcast on any radio station (feasibility)?*

The three co-founders began by focusing on *desirability* and *viability*. They wanted to prove that there was both a strong need from listeners and also a compelling business proposition for radio stations and advertisers *before* they invested resources to solve the technical and workflow challenges. However, they already had an early belief that the core technology (audio recognition) was feasible, based on the availability of music recognition apps allowing users to identify songs they hear on the radio or anywhere else. After many experiments, observations and conversations with listeners and radio broadcasters, the three friends were sufficiently convinced that this was a valuable opportunity to create a start-up venture, and AirShr was born.

At this point, they began to prototype the technology and user experience to tackle the issue of feasibility.

It was clear from the outset that this digital service would require input from many stakeholders within the radio industry, including presenters, sales people, content producers, technical staff and advertising agencies. There was also a need to extract radio program metadata from multiple, disparate sources. The co-founders had no background in radio, so they realised they would need to collaborate closely with radio industry experts.

The early prototype helped them to convince the management of a radio station to pilot AirShr. Indeed, it would have been much harder – or perhaps even impossible – to convince management to partner with AirShr if the idea had been presented as a PowerPoint presentation because nothing similar on the market had yet existed. AirShr needed to demonstrate the experience to the radio station so they could understand how it would benefit their listeners and their business. On the basis of the demonstration, radio station management gave the AirShr co-founders access to their team and their data, and collaborated closely with them over the ensuing twelve months.

At AirShr, 'feasibility' means 'anything required to deliver the service'. It's a broad definition that goes beyond technology and access to include data broadcasting. It also includes radio station workflows to be able to provide them with their data and enhance each radio moment with rich media content. It was only by working with the radio station that AirShr founders could uncover all the factors required to deliver their service. The elements of feasibility were discovered over time – they were not all apparent up front: *'We didn't know what we needed to know until we needed it.'* Nonetheless, the co-founders did conduct extensive industry research before establishing AirShr; they learned as much as possible about the context before investing in the opportunity they had identified.

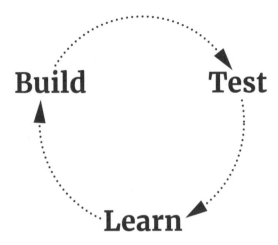

Build

Test

Learn

Figure 6.9: A lean start-up approach

The AirShr founders applied a very simple iterative approach to design and development, the so-called 'lean' start-up approach (see Figure 6.9). In each iteration, they defined what they wanted to achieve. Then they would build a version of the technology and test it with listeners and radio staff to identify issues and insights, which they applied to the next revision. This approach helped them to rapidly uncover and address technical and workflow (feasibility) requirements.

It would have been very difficult to predict these requirements up front.

Feasibility questions asked in every iteration:
- Does the technology deliver our user experience targets?
- Are we getting the right data from the radio station?
- Can the radio station cope with the additional workflow?

As the AirShr co-founders embarked on this journey, they knew what they wanted to achieve. However, they did not know *how* they were going to achieve it – they had no idea of its ultimate feasibility. Although they encountered many technology and workflow roadblocks along the way, the multidisciplinary team's shared vision and focus ensured that they worked together to find a solution to each problem.

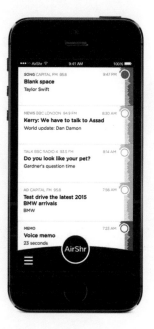

1. Listener test

A basic voice recorder app to measure how often listeners hear something on the radio that they want to remember. Testers kept this app open while driving, and tapped the button whenever they heard something they wanted to keep.

2. Proof of concept

The radio data was faked by manually entering it. This was sufficient to sell the service into a regional radio station who would conduct the pilot.

3. Regional pilot

Working closely with a small regional radio station, AirShr successfully integrated data and aligned to its workflow. Various methods of promoting AirShr on-air were tested to attract listeners to the platform.

4. Metropolitan launch

The insights from the pilot enabled AirShr to integrate with a much larger metropolitan radio network with much more sophisticated technology. The larger station presented a new set of technical and workflow challenges.

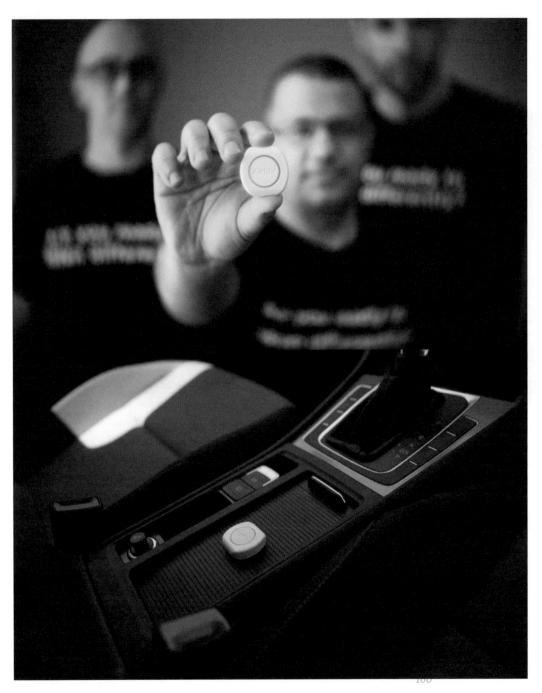

AirShr Bluetooth remote device
Pairs with the driver's smartphone. Drivers simply
tap the button whenever they hear anything
they like. The remote activates the app on their
smartphone to capture the radio segment.

A small, inspired team
The core AirShr team: multi-disciplinary,
collaborative, iterative.

6.4

Conclusion

This chapter provides strategic designers with insights into how to design for feasibility. In order to ensure that identified opportunities are actually implemented, feasibility needs to be explicitly taken into account during the design process. We suggested that to do so, designers may need to do a feasibility audit to establish the types of resources/capabilities that are needed to exploit an opportunity; examine whether the organization actually has those resources and capabilities; and devise an action plan if those resources or capabilities do not exist, or are of insufficient quality to actually implement the opportunity successfully.

As shown in the case studies, a feasibility audit can be done as a one-off, or be conducted in a more continuous, iterative fashion. Fully researching and understanding the feasibility requirements for complex projects may be especially difficult up front. The complex nature of a particular project like AirShr's

digital radio service, for example, made it difficult to fully plan and design using traditional methods. An agile, iterative build-test-learn approach will help strategic designers to uncover feasibility requirements over time. This is what IDEO calls 'building to think'.

Another important message of this chapter is that co-creation with industry experts is of utmost importance to design for feasible innovation. For example, in the AirShr project, constant input from radio station experts was required to guide the design of its technology platform and content workflow. AirShr's solution would not have been feasible without input from these experts. In a similar vein, co-creation with the highly-experienced automotive engineers from the manufacturing company ensured the creation of a product that could be manufactured with little retooling of existing manufacturing capital, which was essential for the company's survival.

About the authors

GERDA GEMSER received her PhD in Management at the Rotterdam School of Management (Erasmus University Rotterdam). Gerda does research on design and innovation management in the creative industries. She has been a visiting scholar at leading research universities, including The Wharton School, the University of Pennsylvania (US) and the Sauder School of Business, University of British Columbia (Canada). Over the last 15 years, she has held assistant and associate professorships at different Dutch universities, including Erasmus University and Delft University of Technology (Faculty of Industrial Design Engineering). She has collaborated with Dutch government, Dutch professional design associations and Dutch industry on different large-scale research projects to examine the role of design in the corporate world. Currently, she is one of five international Professors of Design appointed by RMIT University to further strengthen the university's leadership and expansion of design research. Gerda has published in leading management and design journals *Organization Science*, *Organization Studies*, *Journal of Management*, *Long Range Planning*, *Journal of Product Innovation Management*, *Design Studies* and *International Journal of Design*. She is part of the editorial board of *Journal of Product Innovation Management* and *Journal of Design, Business & Society*.

BLAIR KUYS is Full Professor of Industrial Design at Swinburne University of Technology, Melbourne, Australia, and is currently Department Chair (Head) of Interior Architecture and Industrial Design within the Faculty of Health, Arts and Design. Blair completed a PhD with CSIRO and Swinburne University of Technology in 2010. He is an active researcher and has been instrumental in embedding industrial design research, theories and practice in traditional manufacturing fields to sustain and grow productivity. Blair has a unique ability to work closely with scientists, manufacturers and engineers to legitimise industrial design and the serious impact it can have on an organization. He has over 35 peer-reviewed publications relating to the field of industrial design and product design engineering, and has successfully been awarded over AUD$3.5M in industry-linked research income over the past 5 years. Blair has a close connection with Asia having studied at Hong-Ik University in South Korea and, more recently, he was granted a visiting professorship at Beijing Institute of Technology in China. He continues to supervise a number of local and international PhD candidates all centred on promoting the value of design research on a global scale.

OPHER YOM-TOV is recently appointed as Chief Design Officer at ANZ Banking Group. Before that, Opher (pronounced 'OFF-air') led the Customer Centred Design team at Westpac and BT Financial Group charged with building innovation and design thinking capability, and creating new products, services and experiences for the group. Over the past 8 years, BT Financial Group has launched a number of award-winning insurance, superannuation, investment and financial advice offerings through this approach that have collectively attracted billions of dollars under management. Based on this success, the Westpac Group has committed to scaling the capability across the corporation. Prior to this, Opher spent almost a decade with the global innovation powerhouse IDEO, first in Silicon Valley and then leading their Shanghai start-up office. He has helped develop products, services and innovation capability for corporations such as Apple, Microsoft, Nike, GE, BP, McDonald's, Procter and Gamble, and Pfizer. He advised corporations, large and small, on building and scaling innovation culture and capability, and is a sought-after global public speaker and facilitator of financial service innovation, design thinking and innovation leadership. Opher has also recently co-founded AirShr, a technology venture that aims to bring the magic back to broadcast radio.

References

Amabile, T.M. (1988). A model of creativity and innovation in organizations. *Research in Organizational Behavior*, 10 (1), pp. 123–167.

Australian Government Department of Industry and Science http://www.industry.gov.au/industry/IndustrySectors/automotive/Pages/default.aspx. Accessed 30 March 2015.

Donlon, B.S., and Z. Walmer (2011). Does your organization have the capabilities to execute its strategy? *Balanced Scorecard Report*, 3 (6), November–December, pp. 11–16.

Gemser, G., and H. Perks (2015). Co⊠ Creation with customers: An evolving innovation research field. *Journal of Product Innovation Management*, 32(5), pp. 660–665.

PART IV

Embedding a strategic design project

NERMIN AZABAGIC
IBM Strategy

INGO KARPEN
RMIT University

Making it Count: Linking Design and Viability

7.1

Introduction

The premise of this book is that successful strategic design solutions emerge at the intersection of what is desirable from a customer/user perspective, viable from a business perspective and feasible from a technological/organizational point of view. Blending and aligning these three very different facets for an optimal intersection is not an organic process, and so it needs to be managed explicitly.

From the perspective of managers, the viability aspects of a design solution are often not as robustly developed as the desirability aspects of the solution. For managers, proposed strategic design solutions often pay insufficient attention to likely commercial impacts, leading to, for example, return on investment (ROI) not being sufficiently specified. In other words, managers would like a clear picture of how *commercial value* will be created for the organization by means of the proposed strategic design solution.

Such managerial perceptions and concerns can have significant consequences. Managers may be reluctant to implement the proposed strategic design solution, in particular when other solutions emerge that appear to have a clearer path to investment return. Management may fail to provide further investment in strategic design initiatives, perceiving it as an exercise in improving 'soft' metrics only. Ultimately, management may not appreciate the value that strategic design initiatives and capabilities can bring at an organizational level.

From the perspective of designers, there seems to be recognition that there is a need to increase their knowledge of business and finance. For example, a 2016 'Design in Tech' report from Kleiner Perkins Caufield & Byers found that 86% of current and former design students surveyed wished that 'understanding business and finance' had been a pillar of their education, compared to the 21% who stated that it was.

Managing the viability aspects of a design solution is a nascent concern for many designers. Common pitfalls exist, which we will describe later in the chapter. These common pitfalls are exacerbated by a lack of structured processes, tools and operating models that facilitate better alignment of business viability with desirability and feasibility.

To address this, both larger and smaller design consultancies – such as IDEO, Fjord, and SI Labs – often employ individuals dedicated to lead the viability aspects of design solutions. For the purpose of this chapter, we refer to these as 'business designers' – sometimes also called business strategists – who concentrate their efforts on understanding, shaping, modelling and tracking business success factors and metrics associated with design initiatives.

Business designers typically focus on the firm's business model, ecosystem players and dynamics, industry value drivers and technological trends, the regulatory landscape and cost structures and dependencies, among other aspects – all of which are subsequently used by them during the business casing process, which we will also describe later in the chapter.

If a designer (e.g., service designer, product designer, UX designer, interaction designer) is not interested in developing the complementary skills of a business designer, it is increasingly important to collaborate closely with such a specialist, or otherwise integrate them into the design project team. Even if a designer does not take on the role of a business designer because, for example, another member of the design project team might be responsible for this, any designer who wants to operate at a strategic level, or become a more strategic designer for that matter, needs to at least be able to understand the principles and practices around viability management.

The aims of this chapter are therefore twofold. For those designers who wish to increase their business and commercial acumen, the chapter provides an overview of key challenges and concepts, plus a framework and a real-world case study to show the framework in action. Secondly, for those business designers who would like to improve how they manage the viability aspects of strategic design, we provide a structured approach to managing the 'lifecycle' of strategic design viability, along with tools and recommendations for additional, in-depth resources drawing from the fields of strategy and finance.

7.2

Strategic Design Viability model

What a 'viable' strategic design solution is will naturally depend on the individual circumstances of an organization and the solution proposed. However, general principles can be applied to the concept of viability, namely that any design solution should aim to relate to a genuine (strategic) business opportunity or challenge, generate value in relation to the business opportunity or challenge, and be implemented and recognized as 'successful' by the organization and its key stakeholders.

First, let's start by examining what may be problematic in design projects:

- Business objectives are ill defined. Management has an idea about what they would like to do, but no specific or meaningful success measures are set, which may result in difficulty determining the impact of the design solution on 'hard' financial metrics.
- Designers will explore the problem and potential solutions until they find one that they believe is well suited. Viability is then often fitted to the design solution as an afterthought – that is, after the solution has already been developed and prototyped with customers

(as seen in Figure 7.1 below, in the 'Deliver' stage). Because the solution is attractive to customers and seemingly makes sense to everyone, its viability is often taken for granted. This can be problematic, for example, because the market segment targeted may not be large enough to meet the firm's business objectives, or the price that customers are actually willing to pay may be much lower than anticipated.

- The implementation context might not be sufficiently considered. This leads to challenges realizing the solution, and measures are not in place to monitor how the solution meets key financial milestones.

The key tool to manage the viability of a strategic design initiative is a *business case*. While the term business case is sometimes used synonymously with the term 'business plan', generally a business case can be defined as a justification for a proposed undertaking on the basis of its expected commercial benefit. Business casing typically involves financial modelling, which can be defined as translating a set of hypotheses (assumptions) about the behaviour of

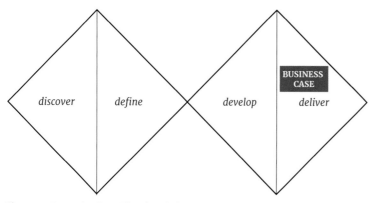

Figure 7.1: Conventional consideration of a business case in the later stages of the design process

markets or customers into numerical predictions and measurable outcomes. While there are many techniques to model out future returns, most of them are not well suited to innovation projects. The challenge when designing a new business model, a new offering or a new experience is that existing parameters cannot be used and new assumptions often have to be made.

One 'assumption-based planning' technique, which is better suited to innovation initiatives, is Discovery-Driven Planning (DDP) (McGrath and MacMillan, 2009). Enhancements to the technique have been provided by Van Putten and MacMillan (2009), who call their extended approach 'Opportunity Engineering' (OE). For those designers who wish to focus on business and financial modelling skills in their work, the suggested books above on DDP and OE will provide further instructions.

For a high level demonstration of how these techniques can be practically applied, we will work through a real-life example below by applying the key practices of DDP, as well as the fields of Strategy and Finance, aligning them to the well-known 'Double Diamond' design process by the Design Council UK.

Case study

Scenario:
For this case study, we will use the pseudonym Oz Bank to represent a large player in the Australian financial services market providing a comprehensive range of banking and wealth management solutions. Oz Bank would like to develop new financial services for female entrepreneurs to gain greater market share within this growing customer segment.

7.3

Step 1 – Setting up the business casing process

Recommended Approach: 5 Key Steps
The business casing process can start even before the design process, and continues into the implementation phase of the design solution(s), as illustrated in Figure 7.2.

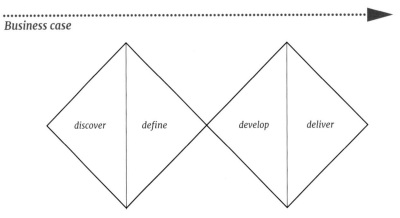

Business case

discover define develop deliver

Figure 7.2: Consideration of financial conditions from the beginning of the design process

Understanding the Business Landscape

Before commencing the business case process, it is important for the (business) designer to understand the business landscape – including extant business models, trends, regulations, industry players and so on.

We can illustrate this practice through our Oz Bank case study. For example, the business designer would firstly need to research not only the immediate competitors for Oz Bank – their key banking rivals – but also the broader competitive set, which for female entrepreneurs might include venture capitalists, 'angel investors' and 'friends and family'. Furthermore, the business designer will also need to find out how the bank and its competitors currently make money from this segment of customers, what proportion of the bank's overall profits this segment represents and how the segment is growing in proportion to other segments – among other factors – while also considering underlying customer need structures.

Starting with a Business or Financial Objective

Many strategic design engagements will

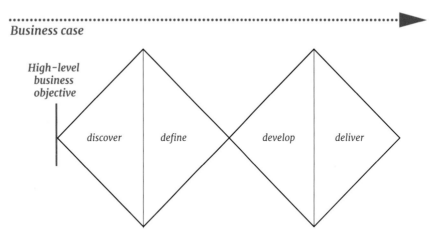

Figure 7.3: Financial conditions and business objectives as frames for the design process

start with an overall business or financial objective that then acts as the catalyst for the strategic design process (see Figure 7.3).

Sometimes higher-order objectives need to be translated into meaningful success targets to start with. Continuing from our Oz Bank example, the business objective can be expressed in several different ways, each quite common in business practice:

Table 7.1: High-level business/financial objectives

Type of Business/Financial Objective	Examples
High-Level Business Objective:	We want to be the #1 Player in the Australian financial services industry for female entrepreneurs.
More specific Business Objective:	We want to increase our market share in the female entrepreneurs segment from 23% to 40% within 3 years.
More Specific Financial Objective:	We want to generate an incremental $100 million in profit between 2017-2019 from the female entrepreneur segment.

Identify and consider any relevant organizational 'hurdles' that must be met: Often organizations will have other specific financial 'hurdles' or concerns, which are thresholds set by the management that must be cleared for projects or initiatives to be approved. These may not be communicated initially, but will need to be identified by the designer. Hurdles can include:

- a 'payback, or break-even period': for example, this financial hurdle might be expressed as 'every project at Oz Bank needs to break even by Year 4', meaning that any initial investment needs to be recouped from the profits by the end of that period;

- ROI, or Net Present Value (NPV) metrics, where an organization might, for example, set a specific percentage as a minimum return that needs to be generated, or set the objective to 'achieve a positive NPV higher than $20 million';

- a specific 'materiality threshold', which might be put in place to prevent the organization from pursuing a large number of small projects; for example, Oz Bank might have the requirement that each project needs to be able to generate a $30 million return by Year 3 to be worth pursuing.

Reverse Profit & Loss Statement
Now that the designer has a better understanding of the overall high-level financial objective (see Table 7.1 above) and is aware of any mandatory hurdles, he or she can start to develop a high-level, future-oriented profit and loss statement (P&L), projecting key financial metrics into the specified timeframe for the solution. The reason why this is important is that it both helps to maintain a focus on key financials, and it helps the designer break down the financial metrics to component parts that will make more sense to them as 'constraints' or parameters for the design solution.

For example, continuing with our Oz Bank case study, let's assume that we are starting with a $100 million profit objective at a high level. We can calculate, as shown in Figure 7.4 below, that to achieve the desired profit, we will need to acquire an additional 12,500 customers to generate revenues of $300 million. The latter includes an average revenue of $24,000 per customer – perhaps generated through interest – and $200 million in costs, which both can be estimated based on Oz Bank historic data, or on average industry statistics, for example.

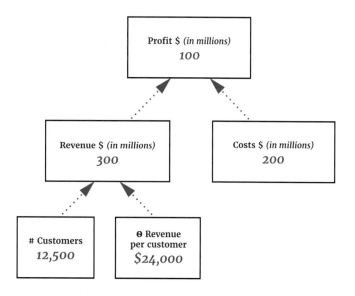

Figure 7.4: Illustrative profit structure

This now becomes a useful parameter for the design process, as we can start comparing it with the size of the existing customer base, the total size of the market, sub-segments of the market and so on. Indeed, breaking down high-level objectives helps the designer assess how realistic the challenge is, and helps to frame design activities accordingly.

Key questions to ask the client organization

- How does your business/industry make money? From which segments/products?
- What are you trying to accomplish with this strategic design initiative? Are there any specific financial outcomes that need to be reached?
- How will we measure success? In what timeframe?
- Are there specific and/or mandatory organizational financial hurdles that need to be met?
- What key assumptions are we starting with?
- Who is the executive sponsor of this initiative?

Key questions to ask yourself as the designer

- Who will manage the 'business casing' of this initiative? Do I have the capacity/capability to do it myself? If not, can the right individual(s) be sourced 'internally' – from the client organization such as strategic or finance experts – or do I need to partner with someone 'external' for this?
- Do I understand the entire business landscape?
- Do I understand the magnitude of the 'ask' (business or financial objectives) in proportion to the client organization's overall business?

7.4

Step 2 – Developing and documenting assumptions

Assumptions are the lifeblood of any future-oriented business case. Indeed, the key question that designers are attempting to answer from a viability perspective for management is *'what do we need to believe for this initiative to be a success?'* which can also be phrased as *'what assumptions can we identify as critical to the success of our business case, and how can we reduce the uncertainty surrounding those assumptions?'*

Therefore, how we manage the underlying assumptions about 'what we believe' needs to be rigorously managed from the outset and throughout the process. These assumptions may revolve around customers, competitors, collaborators, the broader context or the client organization itself. At the beginning of the process, designers will have a few assumptions with a great range of uncertainty or variability; however, as we strategically

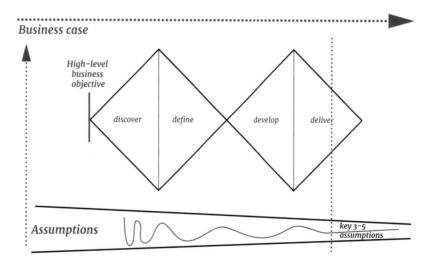

Figure 7.5: Reducing uncertainty of underlying assumptions during the design process

iterate and manage the assumptions throughout the design process – 'we' meaning the designer, business designer and potentially client organization management – even though the number of assumptions might increase, the certainty about the key assumptions should increase significantly. The ultimate objective for the business case is to have a few (3-5) critical assumptions, for which the range of uncertainty has been drastically reduced as the project nears implementation, as illustrated in Figure 7.5.

The assumptions covered in the business case should include not only the 'explicit' assumptions – as in '15% of customers will buy our new service' – but also 'implicit' assumptions about any factors that could affect our initiative – as in 'our competitors will not launch a similar offer in the next 3 years'. The assumptions should be documented methodically, including the source of the assumption, the confidence level – the probability that the assumption is correct – and whether it is an implicit or explicit assumption.

Key questions to ask the client organization
- What assumptions do we need to consider at this stage? Have we considered all relevant assumptions across the entire ecosystem of our initiative: Context, Collaborators, Customers, Company and Competitors (5Cs)?
- What 'blind spots' might we have about 'implicit' assumptions?

Key questions to ask yourself as the designer
- Do I understand the process by which the assumptions are developed?
- What role can I play in developing and validating these assumptions: can I use my 'gut instinct'? experimentation? prototyping?

7.5

Step 3 – Co-creation of the business case, assumptions and solutions

Although in theory, the development of the business case – which involves financial modelling and deriving of assumptions – appears linear across the Double Diamond Process, the business case model grows in detail and complexity as the assumptions are being tested and uncertainties removed. This is demonstrated in Figure 7.6. In simple terms, the tree of factors (also called 'value driver trees') considered to drive the $100 million profit objectives becomes increasingly detailed over time, as represented by the development of the financial model displayed below.

In reality, the process of financial modelling and assumptions testing is non-linear and highly iterative, similar to the design process itself, as illustrated in Figure 7.7.

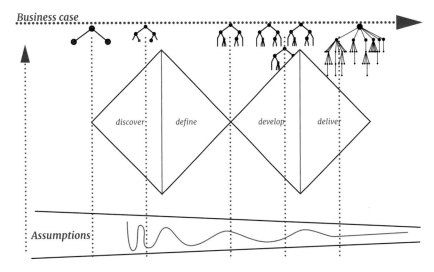

Figure 7.6: Increasing complexity of the business case through the design process as further assumptions are built in, financially modelled and refined.

If the designer does not have the necessary financial modelling skills him-/herself – because he or she has not been trained as a business designer (or business strategist), for example – it is important to collaborate with a relevant expert strategist in the team to develop and iterate a complex business case from the outset and throughout the project. How well the designer works together with his business counterpart on developing the financial model, assumptions, prototypes and the solutions ultimately chosen is the key to success for the client organization. The intersects between the designer and the potential business designer need to be frequent, mutually re-enforcing and exploratory in nature, which is how they will find the optimal nexus of what is both viable and desirable. The process of intersecting is illustrated in Figure 7.8. Intersecting is crucial to how the assumptions are iterated and tested, how the financial model is built and how the prototypes and solutions are developed and designed.

To facilitate this process, it is recommended that designers and their business counterparts are co-located throughout the design process, so that conversations and iterations (intersects) can occur organically, rather than just at key stages of the design process. The designer might, for example, uncover some insight or a user archetype that might be interesting to explore further, and raise it with the business designer to test the idea for viability. Conversely, the business designer might discover through their analysis some market or segment opportunities (or constraints) that need to be further tested by the designer. While it would be impossible to illustrate every 'intersect' that normally would (and should) occur, we will use the same Oz Bank example to illustrate a couple of scenarios at different stages of the Double Diamond model.

DISCOVERY STAGE: Business Designer to Designer Intersect
Let's assume that the business designer is working through the market and segment composition in more detail to understand the context of the female entrepreneurship market. They have uncovered that while female entrepreneurs are just as likely to be approved for a business loan as males, a much smaller proportion of them

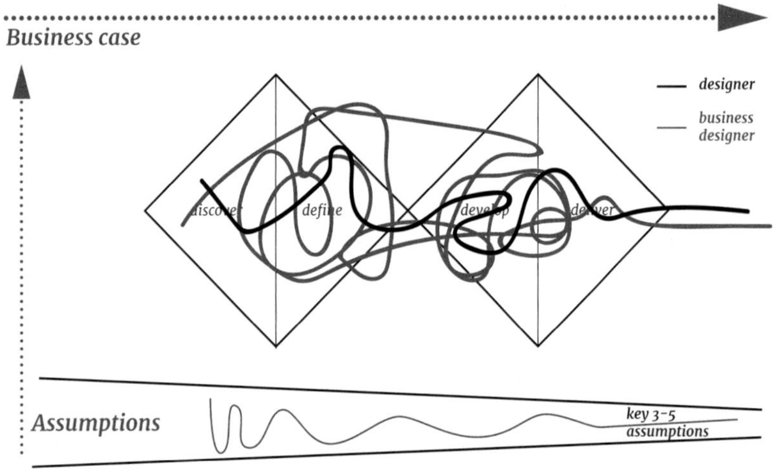

Figure 7.7: Nonlinear assumptions testing

(17%) than males (48%) goes to a bank for financing in the first place, instead relying on other sources of business financing. The business designer now initiates a conversation about how the underlying motivations and feelings those female entrepreneurs have about business financing and the role that the banks play (or do not play) could be explored further.

As a result, the designer might conduct some ethnographic research with female entrepreneurs at their home, or observe them when they go to the bank for a business financing conversation.

DISCOVER STAGE: Designer to Business Designer Intersect
Let's assume that the designer has come back with deep and rich insights from their ethnographic immersion with customers and non-customers, both females and males. A couple of insights that they would like to introduce to the business designer after their synthesis are: 1) male entrepreneurs rely far more heavily on 'incubators' – support networks for startup companies who need advice and venture capital to get their ideas off the ground. They seek both business coaching and guidance,

and also links to bank and venture capital financing through the incubators. 2) females, in comparison, tend to rely much more heavily on friends and their social network for this type of support. The designer also found that females are seen as having a different 'risk' profile from the bank's perspective when compared to men, as they earn less on average, tend to have less assets and have periods out of employment due to child birth and care. At the same time, females seem more risk averse and more careful with spending decisions. The bank only tends to look at their 'assets' with the bank, rather than seeing them as businesses – in terms of

their cash flow or projected potential, or as individuals – in terms of their capability, knowledge and skills.
As a result of these insights, the business designer will now explore the business model and economics of the 'incubator' model in detail, to understand the underlying value drivers and assumptions, and explore Oz Bank's lending criteria for business loans in detail. They will also seek to understand the current risk assessment criteria that the bank uses, and start modelling how the relaxation of the various criteria would impact the risk/return trade-offs.

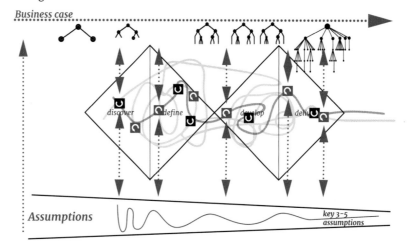

Figure 7.8: Illustrative interaction points between the designer and business designer/financial modeller during the design process

DEVELOP STAGE: Business Designer to Designer Intersect

Let's assume that, based on the analysis and financial modelling the business designer has conducted, there are two potentially viable opportunities taken from an initially much broader list of ideas:

1. **An Oz Bank-run incubator concept** that would target female entrepreneurs, and offer them the services they need with a potential link into business finance if/when required. For this financial model prototype to work, the key assumptions are:
   a. Oz Bank needs to attract an additional 1.5% (or just over 10,000) of new female entrepreneurs per year; and
   b. Oz Bank needs to convert 35% of those customers to its business loan product, and another 25% to its business credit card offer, with an assumed average revenue of $24,000 per year.

2. **A special 'female-friendly' business loan product concept**, which would use very different lending criteria than a typical bank risk assessment:
   a. Risk assessment would include not only the assets held at the bank, but also an assessment of the overall individual and the overall business, including cash flow and projected growth potential; and
   b. An additional 15,000 customers are assumed to apply for this product, with an assumed approval rate of 80%, with a slightly higher revenue potential ($27,000) but also a slightly higher default rate (5% compared to the current 2%). This scenario would also include $5 million in marketing costs to promote the offer and attract new customers into the bank.

With these clear assumptions, the designer can now start prototyping, testing, refining and iterating the concepts with potential target customers that will increase the desirability of this solution.

DEVELOP STAGE: Designer to Business Designer Intersect

Let's assume that the designer has now extensively tested the concept solutions with customers. They debrief with the business designer/strategist about their findings:

1. **Prototype Solution 1:** The appeal of the solution was high, especially with female entrepreneurs who were in the 'growth' stage of their businesses. Also, they found that there was potential for the Incubators to offer a much wider range of services, which could potentially include accounting, financial planning, HR consulting and leadership coaching services.

2. **Prototype Solution 2:** The appeal of the product solution with 'holistic' lending criteria was moderately high; however, getting female entrepreneurs to think

differently about Oz Bank was going to be a challenge, given negative brand associations among female entrepreneurs – even with a sizeable marketing budget. They wondered whether a 'sub-brand' with a stand-alone proposition could work better here, as there would be no pre-existing brand associations for the customers, even though it might be more costly to set up initially.

Now the business designer can start to incorporate the iterations to the prototype solutions into the financial model, and assess viability through scenario modelling.

While this is only a snapshot across a couple of stages of the design process, it hopefully demonstrates how the 'intersects' and timely collaboration between the designer and the business designer or strategist can help to improve both the desirability and viability of the solutions, with feasibility being another important consideration throughout the process.

Key questions to ask yourself
- How can we tighten the collaboration between the designer and the business designer?
- What financial parameters can the business designer provide to the designer that would be helpful constrains for the design process?
- From business designer to designer: how can I help to quantify the insights and opportunities you are uncovering and developing?
- As a designer: How can I work closely with someone who will likely have a very different mindset and outlook from my own?
- From designer to business designer: How can I help to test the key assumptions? What are the opportunities uncovered by the financial modelling and how could we explore and validate them further?

7.6

Step 4 – Identifying key sensitivities for the implementation phase

Determine critical assumptions

As introduced earlier, the ultimate objective for a business case is to have a few (3-5) critical assumptions, for which the range of uncertainty has been drastically reduced. At this point in the process, we have built out our financial model, which can contain dozens, and often hundreds of assumptions, which are linked together with calculations to produce a 'reverse profit and loss' statement. To help identify those assumptions that are the most critical to the business case being achieved, the business designer – possibly assisted by a financial modeller – is able to use sophisticated financial analysis techniques, such as 'Monte-Carlo simulations', to identify 'key sensitivities'. As a result of this analysis, they will be able to say that, for example, 'if the following three key assumptions are achieved within the assumed ranges, there is an 80% likelihood of the business case being achieved', or that 'for every 1% we deviate from this key assumption, it will impact our business case by $150,000'. These can be powerful messages for senior management when presenting the business case for endorsement, while also providing clarity to the implementation phase, as the design team now knows the critical parameters to focus on achieving, and can design the implementation plan accordingly.

Figure 7.9: Consideration of the measurement plan

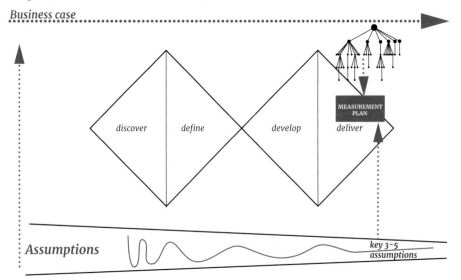

Business case

discover   *define*   *develop*   *deliver*

MEASUREMENT PLAN

Assumptions   key 3–5 assumptions

- Key milestones, and remediation plans if milestones or assumption ranges are not reached, including when designers will need to re-engage in the project;
- Roles and responsibilities for the measurements; and
- An assessment of how the ongoing management of the business case will be conducted, including any subsequent revisions of the measurement plan.

Develop a Design Measurement Plan
A key instrument to design and monitor a successful implementation and subsequent value realization is a design measurement plan, which comes to life in the final phase of the Double Diamond model as shown in Figure 7.9 above. A good measurement plan should be detailed, and contain:

- Critical assumptions and ranges being tested or validated in each milestone period;

Continuing on with the same Oz Bank example, let's assume that the key elements of a simple design measurement plan at a high level would include the following elements, as illustrated in Table 7.2:

Table 7.2: Illustrative elements of a design measurement plan

Measurement	Assumption	Range	Timing	Risk Mitigation
Ability to roll-out/scale	5 incubators at scale	4-6 incubators running at scale	Within first 6 months	Strong project & change management
Customer acquisition	1000 customers per quarter	800-1200	Within first 3 months	Designer involved and observing initial customer conversations at key intervals
Split of revenues	50% Business Financing 30% FP and Accounting 20% Other		Within first 3 months	Financial dashboard Customer feedback of usefulness at 1 and 2 months
Revenues	$26K	$22-29K	Within first 6 months	Conduct financial analysis at 3 months

Codify key Design features

'Design dilution' through implementation is where a great design fails to realize its potential, because the implementation takes away the 'essence' of what made the design great in the first place in its quest to save costs, gain internal approvals or get to market quickly. Therefore, key design features need to be codified for implementation considerations – in other words, designers need to bottle the 'essence of design'. This can be done in different formats, either as part of the design measurement plan, or the final design deliverable, but the idea is to ensure that key design features – those that are non-negotiable – are prescribed in some detail. It is important for the designer to identify which components of the solution create the desired experience and the business value crucial to the success of the solution.

EXAMPLE:

Continuing from our previous Oz Bank example, let's assume that the key design feature that needs to be coded here is the female and child 'friendliness' of the incubator space. The customer testing had found that it was really important for female entrepreneurs to be able to come in and speak with their business coaches at any time, without having to worry about childcare, or whether the environment would be 'unfriendly' to them and their children. The strategic designer should therefore codify what about the space makes the target customers feel the way that we want them to feel for the proposition to work.

Key questions to ask yourself
- What are the 3-5 critical assumptions that have the largest impact on our business case, and what are the ranges that we need to achieve?
- What happens if we don't achieve those ranges – which aspects, how and when will we change our assumptions, solutions and business case?
- What are the key design features of our solution that are essential to be preserved through the implementation phase?
- When does the designer need to revisit the key elements of their design in the implementation stage?

7.7

Step 5: Evaluate success of the design initiative

The key metric that managers can use to evaluate the success or performance of a particular design initiative might be the return on investment (ROI). Strategic design ROI can be viewed from 2 perspectives – the 'micro' perspective, which asks 'what is the ROI of the specific strategic design initiative?' and the 'macro' perspective, which asks 'what is the overall ROI of strategic design?' As this chapter is about initiative-level viability, we focus on micro-level outcomes.

Micro (initiative or project) level

The question of how much value strategic design offers is often raised by management. Strategic design, as prescribed by this book, requires a demonstration of accountability related to design initiatives. One way of showing accountable practices is by way of the ROI of the overall design initiative, calculated using the key metrics in the business case – projected revenues and costs – in a standard ROI calculation. However, often organization- and project-specific KPIs are equally important to track the degree to which the design solution helps achieve initial goals and triggers success drivers.

The costs for any strategic design resources, whether internal or external, should be accounted for in the overall project budget, and funded as per the project funding protocol of the individual organization. The point here is that deploying strategic design resources during the initiative is simply 'business as usual' when it comes to early-stage innovation or strategic design related projects, in the same way that legal, finance, marketing and other parts of the organization are involved in the operationalization of the initiatives.

7.8

Conclusion

This chapter has demonstrated how an existing gap between managers and designers can be closed by better managing the viability aspects of strategic design solutions. A model for managing viability has been provided, with practical tools, a high-level case study and further resources helping designers better understand and implement viability considerations.

Importantly, the core principle highlighted and embedded in the approach is one of integration, whereby viability and desirability (along with feasibility) are managed and traded off in a holistic, iterative and fully collaborative fashion throughout the lifecycle of the design initiative. Viability extends beyond its own commercial context, and can help frame and quantify how 'valuable' solutions might be, not only for customers, but indeed for the broader organization, community and society.

Practical implications for those who are in-house designers – depending on personal aspirations and preferences – are to either invest in developing their own commercial skills towards becoming business designers, or to identify individual(s) within the organization who have the requisite skills to manage the viability aspects of the strategic design initiatives, either formally or informally. Design agencies have a similar choice – improve their own business and finance skills or bring in the expertise through partnering with a specialist firm or individual.

Using business-casing techniques suggested here, it is possible to evaluate different options, iterate the ideas in a plan and encourage experimentation at the lowest possible cost. When combined with the exploratory nature of design in terms of generating what is desirable, results can be synergistic and 'greater than the sum of their parts'. The key to achieving this effect is managing the business and design processes throughout the initiative, in concert and in an iterative fashion, as illustrated here.

About the authors

NERMIN AZABAGIC is a strategist with over 18 years of international corporate experience. His career has spanned a variety of client-side and service-side organisations, including Wunderman, AMP, Westpac and Accenture. He is currently a Strategy Lead at IBM Interactive Experience, and consults on Innovation, Digital Strategy & Transformation and Business Design. An ambidextrous thinker, he operates at the intersection of business and design to drive value for firms through innovation. His corporate experience has included working on designing and launching successful new business models, services and products, as well as award-winning new digital and offline customer experiences. He believes inter-disciplinary collaboration is key in developing successful design-led, commercially viable propositions.

Nermin holds a BCom in Management from Ryerson University in Toronto, an Executive MBA from University of New South Wales in Sydney (AGSM) and is currently completing a PhD at RMIT in Melbourne, where his research explores the combination of design thinking and financial modelling in a service innovation context.

INGO KARPEN is an Associate Professor and cross-disciplinary researcher in Marketing, Strategy, and Design at RMIT University, Melbourne. Ingo is also a visiting Professor at Copenhagen Business School. In his research, Ingo focuses on drawing on service and design principles to better understand and inform value co-creation strategies in service systems; measuring and investigating the interplay of service-driving organizational design and user experience design; and managing service systems and human relations towards more engaging experience processes and experience outcomes. Ingo collaborates with international business partners across industries to facilitate knowledge generation for the betterment of business and society. He has published in the *Journal of Service Research, Journal of Retailing, Journal of Business Research, Marketing Theory, Journal of Strategic Marketing, Journal of Travel Research, Journal of Service Theory and Practice* and *International Marketing Review*. He is a recipient of several national and international awards for his teaching and research.

References

McGrath, R., & MacMillan, I. (2009). *Discovery-driven growth*.

Putten, A., & MacMillan, I. (2009). *Unlocking opportunities for growth*. Upper Saddle River, N.J.: Wharton School Pub.

www.kpcb.com, K. (2016). *Design in Tech Report 2016. Kpcb.com*. Retrieved 4 April 2016, from http://www.kpcb.com/blog/design-in-tech-report-2016

INGO KARPEN
RMIT University

ONNO VAN DER VEEN
Ideate

YOKO AKAMA
RMIT University

Lasting Design Impact Through Capacity Building

8.1

Introduction

Most designers strive to achieve some form of lasting impact – perhaps by implementing unique and innovative design proposals, or through changes they inspire within the client organization and among its stakeholders. In the following chapter, we take a closer look at how these practices serve to 'embed' design in today's organizations.

To us, the designer's *mindset* – or worldview – is an important factor for success. We like to differentiate between what we call a 'problem-solving mindset' and a 'capacity-building mindset'. The former is a relic from the earlier days of conventional design that emphasizes a linear model of analysis and synthesis, and assumes that problems are definable and have predictable conditions. However, as many of today's problems are of a 'wicked' nature, and tried and tested solutions no longer satisfy the ever-evolving needs of stakeholders and the environment, complexity and

indeterminacy can be expected during any process of design development. In fact, although organizations possess extensive knowledge of their chosen fields, many may not have yet developed the designer's capacity to see the larger picture, and as a result, the design solutions they seek cannot satisfy complex problems with no single 'right' answer. When designing within this context, we believe that maintaining and fostering a capacity-building mindset is a meaningful strategy of the designer. And even when a problem is relatively narrow and specific, over time the client organization will derive significant benefit from designers' efforts to cultivate design skills and capacities that will serve the organization beyond the current problem or project.

A capacity-building mindset values local, contextual knowledge and competencies, and strives to encourage organizations to innovatively draw upon their 'creative, organizational capabilities

and entrepreneurship, and therefore [be] capable of figuring out, enhancing and managing new solutions' (Manzini & Rizzo 2011, p. 201). As capacity-builders, designers come to the client as coaches, educators and facilitators, rather than purely as problem solvers, and as such they have a vested interest in enabling stakeholders' use of design tools and approaches – especially organizations undergoing cultural change. The capacity-building mindset aims to prevent organizational overreliance on the designer to solve a 'problem'

– and demonstrates how designerly attitudes, values, skills and tools can be embraced beyond a specific project once the designer's job is done. What might be initially considered as 'strange' or 'unfamiliar', designerly thinking and practice can become an internalised, common approach understood by designers and organizations alike. Burns and colleagues (2006, p. 21) refer to this as 'transformation design [that] seeks to leave behind not only the shape of a new solution, but the tools, skills and organizational capacity for ongoing

change'. The following chapter will reflect on possible strategies and approaches that strategic designers can draw upon to help embed design within organizations and more importantly, to transition their practices beyond one-off design projects. Designers with a capacity-building mindset are thus more likely to see themselves – and act as – 'agents of change' who seek to build skills and abilities, not create dependencies. Over time, this attitude will embed design throughout organizational units and departments. Arguably, the bigger and more complex the client organization – in terms of employee number, or geographical spread – the harder it is for designers to achieve a lasting impact across the organization. Often designers focus on a specific business unit or department to start with. Successful initial projects can then translate into follow-up projects in different organizational areas.

So what can designers do to facilitate capacity building? Working with stakeholders, particularly client employees, to help them understand relevant design tools and techniques is a core element; helping them understand how and why designers think the way they do is another important aspect. Throughout this book you will find references to designer practices in which specific tools and techniques are being used. As a complement to the previous chapters, this chapter condenses underlying ways of designerly thinking into a set of design principles based on the work of the first author and colleagues (Karpen, Gemser and Calabretta, 2017). We argue that these design principles have implications beyond design practice. When they are brought to life through education, facilitation and co-creative interventions, they not only help an organization contribute to the design process more effectively, but these principles – and the experience the organization acquires by learning how to apply them – also function as important drivers of transformative design, because their application guides and (re)orients the culture of the client organization toward mutual development and innovation.

8.2

Design principles

In this section, we will crystallise core design principles that support respective capacity-building, and help client organizations go on a journey that fosters designerly thinking and practice. Table 8.1 outlines these principles and their theoretically-driven reasoning, which we explain further below.

Table 8.1: Design Principles (based on Karpen, Gemser and Calabretta, 2017)

Design Principle	Conceptual Explanation
Make it about people!	Design is human and meaning centred in nature
It's a team sport!	Design is co-creative and inclusive in nature
Have a better-bias!	Design is transformative and betterment-oriented in nature
Push for experimental uncovering!	Design is emergent and experimental in nature
Enable a great story!	Design is explicative and experiental in nature
See the bigger picture!	Design is holistic and contextual in nature

1) *Make it about people:*
Design is human- and meaning-centred.

Inherently, design is oriented neither toward products nor technology. These dispositions are only the means to an end, which is to shape meaning and facilitate experiences and outcomes that are human-centred (Krippendorff, 2006). The human needs and desires addressed by design tend to take precedence over concerns for viability and feasibility. While these cannot be neglected (as outlined in Chapters 6 and 7), the insights that shape designs often revolve around feelings, meanings, social and cultural contexts and practices. Because designing aims to change our futures or intervene in our lives, designers must carefully consider the impact and implications of their ideas. This care forms the basis upon which design can become desirable within technological or financial constraints. In sum, people, such as customers and users, are of primary concern.

2) *It's a team sport:*
Design is co-creative and inclusive.

Designing is essentially social and relational. Participation and inclusion in the design process can unleash stakeholders' creative potential – even non-customers and 'peripheral' contributors can generate a variety of useful, pertinent insights and ideas. Comparing and collating these different stakeholder interactions and expectations, including from stakeholders at the periphery of the market (particularly non-customers), can contribute in varying degrees to design processes

3) Have a 'better-bias':
Design is transformative and betterment-oriented.

and outcomes. The designer models and inspires openness to a diversity of experiences, views and ideas through ongoing exchanges with stakeholders that stimulate and integrate their collective creative power. Indeed, the collaborative and integrative nature of co-design can support the empowerment and commitment of various stakeholders, which reflects the transdisciplinary character of design more generally, and its appreciation for integrating multiple perspectives.

Design is a significant mode of cultural and economic value creation, playing a central role in shaping and informing the ways people work, live and imagine their futures. However, rather than evaluating designs as 'right' or 'wrong', 'good' or 'bad', less value-laden questions and discussion should take place to ask what kind of society, culture and environment design contributes toward, and more importantly, what 'betterment' might mean, for whom, and in what context. Given that design is

responsive to dynamic and contingent contexts, designers must listen, reflect, seek opportunities to question the impact of their designs, and to involve stakeholders in the co-design and negotiation of desired futures. This means that design outcomes need to be considered with care, in terms of their long-term and multi-layered impact on the environment and society. A mutually shared concern for improvement can guide awareness of how design is implicated and embedded.

4) Push for experimental uncovering:

Design is emergent and experimental.

Designing evolves through iteration and experimentation, which is influenced by ongoing feedback and reflection. The design process can often be characterised as stages of exploration of the diverging, and realisation of the converging, to progressively refine the problem and propositional space (Cross, 2006). Rather than relying on linear processes, design thus builds on continuous iterations that include reframings of complex problems and speculations. It involves trial and error, purposeful seeking, and playing and experimenting with ideas and prototypes without fear of failing. This experimental play is important to stimulate novel ideas, and carve out a creative environment in which those ideas can thrive and deep learning can occur. At the same time, designers must think intuitively, beyond empirical evidence, to determine the potential a proposition has to address contextual conditions. This abductive approach characterises the emergent nature of design, whereby problems, ideations and processes co-evolve.

5) Enable a great story and make it feel real:

Design is explicative and experiential.

Design projects are often shrouded in fuzzy conditions at the beginning and/or throughout the entire process. Problems might be causally ambiguous and complex, and the antecedents and consequences of these problems may be difficult to elucidate and isolate. However, design stresses the importance of making the intangible tangible, explicative and understandable so that stakeholders can experience design propositions by proxy, even if these are never resolved into a final manifestation. Using prototypes, visualizations and storytelling, among other approaches, designers can help stakeholders feel, hear, see, touch, taste and embody what is being speculated

6) See the bigger picture:

Design is holistic and contextual.

upon, which will enable the development of more concrete experiences. Design can make the subconscious conscious – it leverages various sensorial aspects to imagine and communicate alternatives. Experiential techniques encourage a diversity of rich encounters, and the 'realness' of these interactions drives the iteration process more concretely toward fulfilling the combined vision of the stakeholders involved.

Since designing takes place in interconnected systems, changing one element is likely to affect other elements in the system. For instance, if an organization changes the components and quality of its smartphone, it is likely to have a direct impact on various suppliers, customers and other stakeholders. While customers might benefit from improved usability, suppliers and producers will likely have to change their materials and processes to fit the requirements of the new product. In the same way, at a community level, a change in policy could have a number of flow-on effects across different stakeholder groups. Hence, designers must aim to

understand how and why different kinds of stakeholders and resources are integrated, and how design can impact the resources, relations, systems and stakeholders and their actions, directly and indirectly. This will prevent design or its agency being seen as isolated and compartmentalized, and will enable insights that beneficially leverage or avoid negative systemic effects because they consider the holistic context that determines an outcome.

While these design principles are theoretically relevant across contexts, how can designers help organizations to embrace these principles?

8.3

Leveraging and embedding the design principles in the client organization: Designers as coaches

Designers often satisfy a dual goal: to provide a service that responds to a specific 'problem' and to help the client organization learn how to use or leverage designerly thinking and tools. To this end, designers need to put on both a designer hat and an educator hat – educating organizations can create the cohesion necessary for designers to effectively inspire and direct the combined efforts of every stakeholder involved.

'Some of the best designers are the ones who are actually good teachers, because they help the client understand and value what they are doing. They don't just deliver a pretty picture. It's the insights behind the picture. And to get somebody to value the insight, they actually have to know a lot more about what and why you have done something. So [designers] light the fire, and get the client excited about going on this journey together', says Opher Yom-Tov, Chief Design Officer at ANZ Banking Group.

Understanding this dual role of practitioner and educator is the crucial first step toward embedding designerly approaches in a client organization. For example, designers can initiate kick-off workshops to stimulate excitement within the organization, and build momentum for design projects. This might take the form of a 'crash course in human-centred design' aimed at executives, managers, decision makers and employees alike, to secure engagement across departments while members experience important steps in the design process first-hand. Ideally, both problem owners and project sponsors should also participate in addition to a range of other stakeholders. The sponsor is the person paying the bills – and hence who cares about value for money – and his or her drives can be identical or different to the 'owner' of the problem or project, whose domain of activity executes and needs to benefit from the proposal. These practices reflect the design principles discussed earlier – making it about people and treating design projects as a team sport to empower the range of stakeholders involved. The workshops can function as experiential gateways to enable great stories and uncover alternative ways of doing things, as we will illustrate in the following paragraphs.

As people in different roles across different departments may potentially speak different business languages, these workshops are an extremely critical opportunity to build the basis for shared understanding and excitement. Designers actively involve employees of the client organization in the design process. Staff members can learn qualitative user research techniques (for example, recruiting, interviewing, synthesizing), or they can be invited to create personas or map out customer journeys. In one case, a designer helped the staff of an automotive supplier to conduct stakeholder research, which involved them crafting targeted and relevant questions during interviews with car mechanics and undertaking observations to draw out various customer perspectives. Through these newly-learned techniques, the automotive client organization was able to address shortcomings in their previous notions of the producer-consumer relationship and develop insights and clearly connected relationships. Design collaboration can help organizations to transition toward being more customer- or user-centric. With increasing experience and sufficient training, client stakeholders can drive or even lead the application of design tools, so that the organization can become a self-sufficient system that is excited about their design capabilities, and thus their ability to recognize, address and produce despite the intrinsic complexity of their changing operations.

In addition to convincing key employees to actively take part in all the steps of a design process, designers can also translate the findings of user research into visualizations that paint a vivid customer picture. In one recent project, this included printing human-sized personas distributed throughout the client organization to continuously inform and remind employees of customer feedback, needs and contexts. Short video clips can be equally as powerful, by bringing customer motives, barriers and other types of relevant insights to life. Giving voice and thus animating customer (and other) stakeholder perspectives is an impressive and effective way to educate management. In one workshop a designer asked employees to write down one observation from their customer interviews per sticky note, and attach these to a wall. Employees were then asked to tell a story that made sense of their observations. After sharing their insights, employees were then asked to allocate the Post-its into emerging thematic groups during a silent ordering exercise, ultimately helping them to distil and synthesise key insights. These examples demonstrate how design can bring a more human-centred approach to the design process, motivate people to collaborate in that process and teach them concrete and explicit ways to maintain a customer-focused approach themselves on their own – related to design principles 1, 4 and 5.

Although enabling employees to have a more active say at various stages of the design process can impart a real sense of empowerment, designers can sometimes exhibit a 'not-invented-here' attitude. This means rejecting an idea, or judging other stakeholders' proposals too critically because they have not been proposed by the designers themselves, and hence seem not worthy of objective consideration and/or appear to not deserve any credit, let alone praise. This is when ego becomes an issue. As much as organizations and leaders need to be aware of this with regards to ideas generated by people 'external' to the organization, designers also need to take care not to fall into a similar trap. To help an organization embrace design, endorsement of and support for advancing client-based proposals toward implementation leads to feelings of ownership. The latter is essential for human motivation. Employees are likely to care more about the relevance and practice of design when they have been involved in the process, being able to contribute, feeling heard and valued, and ultimately their ideas or suggestions respected or even implemented. While a specific proposal during the co-creation process might be discarded due to a lack of desirability, feasibility and/or viability, it is important to give a detailed 'why not' for that decision. Co-creating stakeholders need decision-making transparency, so that they may learn to avoid similar mistakes in the future and to help them feel like valued contributors. A designer's role can again be that of a coach, by encouraging staff to decouple their personal feelings from their rejected proposals, and eventually enhancing their faculties of judgement to automatically utilize the lenses of desirability, feasibility and viability. While designers cannot necessarily turn client employees into designers overnight, they can, however, build an important foundation that triggers curiosity in and appreciation for design. Thereby, designers can exceed the constraints of practical logic and tap into the emotional dimensions of the employees and other stakeholders, with the ultimate goal of creating emotionally rich contexts and experiences for customers. With a human touch and a wider focus, employees are more likely to engage in the process, and even become design ambassadors. Identification and selection of those design ambassadors is actually another factor that helps an organization embrace design. 'Design champions' become key promoters of the design process within the client organization and are thus a critical link for the designer; coaching these employees can lead to manifold effects – ambassadors endorse and stimulate designerly thinking, tools and approaches within the organization. Indeed, ambassadors are able to envision the potential intrinsic to the design agency, where others may need more evidence or assurance. However, designers might need to emotionally support design ambassadors through advice and encouragement, as many internal resistances and hurdles can already be present in organizational processes and culture. This can sometimes be frustrating and demoralising for design ambassadors.

HCD DEMAND GREW RAPIDLY

PROJECT

1. STRATEGIC OR VALUABLE
2. FULLY SCOPED
3. RIGHT TEAM FOR RIGHT TIME
4. FUNDING
5. TIME BOXED

APPROACH

6. APPLY AN HCD APPROACH
7. AGREE TO BE CHALLENGED
8. PROVIDE TEAM SPACE (VIRTUAL & PHYSICAL)

THE RULES OF ENGAGEMENT
COMMITMENT
SIGNED
GENERAL MANAGER

COMMITMENT

9. SPONSOR / GM SUPPORT
10. SPONSOR/ GM TIME COMMITMENT
11. INTENT TO INVEST IN THE OUTCOME

© OPHER YOM-TOV
24th JULY 2014

Figure 8.1: Illustrative rules of engagement for Human Centred Design (HCD) projects

Designers thus have an interest in building closer ties with key players across teams within the organization – not just to secure buy-in and ownership, but also to provide much needed mutual support – related to design principle 2. Clarifying which horizontal and vertical unit these ambassadors may be positioned in, through mapping the organization, can be helpful.

Designers often have to deal with changing conditions of an organization and design project – project team members could leave the organization, or be taken off projects to attend other organizational needs/projects, or design ambassadors might step away from their role due to frustrations with the potential challenges they face when promoting design internally. Designers need to be resilient, and ready for the hard work it will take to potentially train or re-educate organizational members. In anticipation of potential changes, designers can define 'rules of engagement' that set expectations for anyone involved in the project. Defining such expectations helps everyone to understand priorities and no-go areas. Rules of engagement frame designers' efforts to ensure successful customer-centric solutions that are desirable, viable and feasible, and to scale human-centred design capability across the business to enable others to practice the approach. Figure 8.1 illustrates one way to do this, taken from a recent design project.

Figure 8.2 outlines some strategic questions to ask in relation to these rules of engagement.

Strategic Questions:

1) Is the design project of strategic importance and value to the business?
2) Is the scope of the design project fully understood?
3) Can you get the right team with the right time commitment?
4) Do you have sufficient funding (or a clear pathway to funding)?
5) Is it realistically timeboxed?

Strategic Questions:

6) Are you committed to applying a HCD approach?
7) Are you ready to let yourself be challenged, and to change course based on findings? Can you set your ego aside?
8) Can you provide the space (physical/virtual) to enable the team to collaborate effectively?

Strategic Questions:

9) Does this design project have full sponsor and decision maker support and buy-in?
10) Will the sponsor and decision maker make the necessary time commitment?
11) Is the business committed to investing in the outcome? Is there commitment to implement?

Figure 8.2: Strategic questions that refine the rules of engagement

8.4

Transformational design and cultural interventions

Designers cultivating a capacity-building mindset must take into account the specifics of any project and its context. A client organization's internal culture is the central context in which designing unfolds, and as such designers need to make themselves keenly aware of its dominant traits. Refining the accuracy of this perception goes hand in hand with supporting the transformation of that culture into one that practices effective design thinking.

As a start, designers can ask important questions such as 'how does the organization work?' This kind of 'cultural auditing' and awareness building helps designers to better anticipate potential hurdles or intuit levers for design that stem from values, common practices and culturally-informed expectations. (Please refer to Chapter 6 for a more detailed list of feasibility success factors.) For instance, the existing culture might be

risk- or failure-averse – any waste of resources and effort must be minimised. Many organizations perform daily routine protocol checks, or large investments might require multiple sign-off stages across decision-making levels, or company expectations around innovation might focus on finding safe solutions with manageable risks. When a designer intentionally sets about exposing these underlying cultural traits, that audit will reveal conditions that would likely make it harder for the organization to embrace certain design principles, or dynamics that could block the application of effective design practices.

While it might be easier for seasoned designers to influence the direction an organization will take, even junior designers can significantly shape the internal context such that sponsors and decision makers are pleasantly surprised by outcomes, and want other organizational areas/problems to follow a similar approach. Basically, a designer can achieve impact through working with people across multiple levels. For example, designers might purposefully seek interaction with managers who are convinced of – or willing to be convinced by – the benefits of design, and so are also willing to push for the development of design capability across the organization. On the other hand, designers might work with specific teams or departments, for instance, convincing the organization of the value of design incrementally and superior outcomes that literally speak for themselves. Often this means convincing employees one-by-one. Ideally, managers will begin to ask themselves 'why is this dynamic not happening over there, in department X or in project Y?' Designers can stimulate a groundswell of support for their techniques among employees and inspire greater engagement throughout the organization by sharing their processes and tools, and regularly showcasing what they are doing. Stakeholders then have a better chance of becoming organizational anthropologists who more completely understand the whos, whats, and whys behind their processes and outputs . . . and behind their successes and failures – related to design principle 1.

Organizations often wait for massive external threats that require a strong and rapid response before making any radical changes to the way they operate. A ground-breaking offering by a competitor, a major financial dependency, a radical shift in technology, a brand-related 'shitstorm' – just to name a few – are all triggers considered severe enough to force internal shifts within company culture, or spark the search for out-of-the-box solutions. While catastrophes may seem like great starting points for innovation, by developing internal awareness within the organization, designers can drive change minus a sense of impending doom. Organizations 'are collections of human beings, with beliefs, emotions, hopes, and fears. Ignoring predictable, and sometimes irrational, reactions is certain to undermine an initiative in the long run. The first step is to identify negative mindsets and seek to change the way people think about how the organization works' (Aronowitz et al., 2015, p. 106). Guiding the organization to adopt designerly principles and practices requires designers to be extremely astute as regards their own cultural awareness – so that intervention processes are appropriately design-driven themselves. Client organizations and their employees need to be taken on an exciting journey, one equal to what the design aims to achieve with customers. A designer's interactions and interventions on-site should also help them determine what motivates employees, what bothers them, and where opportunities exist to create experiences that change perspectives and attitudes, and model new mindsets. Doing so helps employees identify with design-driven organizational change, feel more empowered and co-responsible while contributing momentum to the initiative. For instance, one designer constructed an intervention that had employees map out their existing core beliefs about the firm and its business context, and then asked them to collectively turn each on its head by asking 'what if...?' (see also techniques developed by de Jong and van Dijk, 2015). These newly-defined beliefs led to fresh implications for customer and employee experiences, and concepting of unique outcomes. Compromising beliefs were exposed and challenged, and concrete ways of embracing alternative positions

became apparent – effects which may also serve to map out the bigger picture and include a broader variety of stakeholders, and the impact that the organization has or is seeking within their community.

Ideally, a client organization already has someone like a chief design officer, whose role it is to focus on design and strategic decision-making. Cultural change can be facilitated by external designers, but ideally is supported through internal design ambassadors and a design leader with real authority – like a chief design officer, or a design director. If such a position and person doesn't exist yet within an organization, it might be helpful for the designer to point out the benefits of having one, and potentially even facilitate efforts to recruit one. Ultimately, design shouldn't just be the task of a design leader – it should be the responsibility of every member

of an organization. It is the cultural responsibility of every employee to recognise and be sensitive to customer needs and desires, to hit the alarm bell when customer 'pain points' and market changes emerge, and to understand the impact of an organization's actions on customer experiences. Equipping stakeholders with customer-centred radar via basic customer-experience research is an essential way designers can facilitate cultural change. Customer empathy and a sense of accountability for their needs are central to building a culture that commits to design. For example, designers might ask relevant employees to imagine customer experience, jointly reflect on this, and develop specific key performance indicators together with other employees and management – the process will ensure that employees' priorities are aligned with desired customer experiences.

Designers can support the transition toward cultural change by being open to experiment, even within certain boundaries, including a strong concern for viability and feasibility (please refer to Chapters 6 and 7 for more on this). While such concerns help designers reduce their risk of failure during experimentation and implementation, it is important to emphasise in working with clients that design values continuous change and evolution – and a culture that accepts that designers are 'always in beta mode'. A solution and experience context is never complete when key performance indicators are in constant need of adaptation. Over time, new opportunities emerge – coincidentally or purposefully – to improve the

Figure 8.3: Participatory design methods (Playful Triggers and Scenario Cards) are used in a training course with Australian emergency management staff to develop capacity in a community-centred approach to strengthening disaster resilience (image credit : Yoko Akama)

design; and designers' interactions with organizations can go a long way toward helping them to understand and embrace this perspective. Akama's (2015) work in Australia demonstrates that establishing a multi-organizational and multi-sector approach to building adaptive capacity and resilience to disasters requires the collaboration and training of many stakeholders. We recently used a variety of participatory design methods – see Figure 8.3 – to train and help emergency agencies transition their 'command and control' culture toward a community-centred approach to preparedness, and develop their ability to engage with, share and leverage localised contextual knowledge of the community – in line with design principles 3 and 6.

Ultimately, continuous organizational improvement needs to be guided by a shared purpose and vision. And that purpose and vision, if not already customer experience-centric, needs to be strongly in tune with its core mission and values, the well-being of customers and supportive to the wider community – related to design principles 3 and 6. Many organizations have a written statement that defines their purpose and vision, and this could be inauthentic if their actions do not reflect customer or community-centred considerations. This is why designers are often hired – to heal pain points relative to customer experience. Nevertheless, strategic designers can always initiate discussions about the bigger picture, to ensure that organizational purpose, priorities

and vision are coherently aligned to its performance and stakeholder engagement. Because such statements can be rather static and non-engaging, designers can use their creative abilities to bring the statement to life and make it more understandable, relatable, compelling and meaningful for staff. Throughout and beyond the completion of a design project, designers can help create cultural artefacts that contain meaning-laden reminders, and in doing so help institutionalize design-driven attitudes and practices. Active and shared purpose and vision can create a sense of belonging, provide a moral compass for action and can energise employees and stakeholders to contribute purposefully toward a shared goal.

8.5

Conclusion

Designers can play an important role both for project-related design and strategic organizational design. To live up to the demands of both, approaching clients with a capacity-building mindset is an important pre-condition. As we have shown above, capacity building can be enabled by helping an organization to understand and embrace design principles. As a first step, organizations can experience the six design principles through a designer's coaching, and during collaboration and staged interventions. In turn, and while reflecting in action,

staff can start to embrace the behavioural implications of the design principles, and ideally replicate these in their own practices.

Cultural interventions build long-term foundations for an environment where true designerly thinking and practice can flourish. Teaching directly influences employee abilities and helps enact designerly approaches through enabling greater confidence. The designer then takes on the role of both a design coach – by using and demonstrating design tools – and of a trusted advisor – by developing a shared vision and inspiring cultural changes. Obviously, changing the entire system is more difficult than changing mere experiential processes. Thus designers need to deploy different approaches at different times across different levels so that interventions work with different contexts and conditions. Designers can perforate boundary identities, integrating marketing, strategy, operations and finance. Given the ethics of design, or the desire to contribute meaningfully for the firm and its various stakeholders, principles and practices can also apply in many community contexts, not just organizational ones. For such unbounded community contexts, where complexity is on the rise, a capacity-building approach to design becomes even more important, so that the focal organization can dynamically and competently handle various ongoing problems.

As a final statement, approaching organizations with a capacity-building mindset means that designers themselves need to build their own capacity through self-development, critical reflection and learning. What can I learn from this project? What did I observe that worked well? What did not work well, and why? How might I approach things differently next time? A designer's responsibility to learn never ends. It's central for designers to set aside sufficient time for reflection-in-action, and draw out key insights of their own, so that they enjoy some sense of mutual benefit that can be applied to future projects.

INGO KARPEN is an Associate Professor and cross-disciplinary researcher in Marketing, Strategy, and Design at RMIT University, Melbourne. Ingo is also a visiting Professor at Copenhagen Business School. In his research, Ingo focuses on drawing on service and design principles to better understand and inform value co-creation strategies in service systems; measuring and investigating the interplay of service-driving organizational design and cuser experience design; and managing service systems and human relations towards more engaging experience processes and experience outcomes. Ingo collaborates with international business partners across industries to facilitate knowledge generation for the betterment of business and society. He has published in the *Journal of Service Research, Journal of Retailing, Journal of Business Research, Marketing Theory, Journal of Strategic Marketing, Journal of Travel Research, Journal of Service Theory and Practice* and *International Marketing Review*. He is a recipient of several national and international awards for his teaching and research.

ONNO VAN DER VEEN. With a background as partner of industrial design agency Scope Design & Strategy, Onno van der Veen founded a practice in service design in 2010 called Ideate. At Ideate, a team of service designers address challenges present in a wide variety of industries, including healthcare, mobility, energy and education. The service design approach proves to be of great help to organizations who seek to to become more client- and user-oriented, develop powerful new value propositions and find a path through complex and systemic challenges. Onno and the Ideate team have special expertise in design for behaviour change, designing services that improve patient therapy adherence, and promote fuel-efficient driving or safe bike riding by the elderly. Working in close collaboration with his clients, Onno brings creativity, enthusiasm and drive that inspires teams to go the extra mile an to create optimistic new perspectives. Apart from developing user-centred services, Onno lectures on service design in several masterclass programs.

Dr. YOKO AKAMA is an award-winning design researcher in the School of Media and Communication, and co-leads the Design+Ethnography+Futures research program (http://d-e-futures.com/) at RMIT University, Melbourne. She also established the Design for Social Innovation and Sustainability in Asia-Pacific network (http://desiap.org/). Her Japanese heritage and Zen-informed reflexive practice carve a 'tao' (path) in human-centred design. Her practice is entangled with complex 'wicked problems' that seek to strengthen adaptive capacity for disaster resilience in Australia and Japan, and contribute towards the efforts of Indigenous Nations to enact self-determination and governance. Trained as a communication designer, visualization features strongly in her approach to catalyse learning, imagining and disruption through participatory interactions. She is an Adjunct Fellow of an ecosystem innovation studio, Re:public Japan and Visiting Fellow at the Centre of Excellence in Media Practice, Bournemouth University. She is a recipient of several major research grants in Australia and the UK, and winner of the prestigious Good Design Australia Awards (2014).

References

Akama, Y. (2015), Continuous Re-configuring of Invisible Social Structures, In: *Designing Work, Technology, Organizations and Vice Versa*, Vernon Press, Wilmington, United States.

Aronowitz, S.; De Smet, A. and D. McGinty (2015), Getting Organizational Redesign Right, *McKinsey Quarterly*, 3, 99-109.

Burns, C.; Cottam, H.; Vanstone, C and J. Winhall (2006), Transformation Design, RED Paper 02, Design Council, London.

Cross, N. (2006), *Designerly Ways of Knowing*, Springer, London.

de Jong, and M. van Dijk (2015), Disrupting Beliefs: A New Approach to Business-model Innovation, *McKinsey Quarterly*, 3, 66-75.

Karpen, I.O, Gemser, G. and G. Calabretta (2017), A Multilevel Consideration of Service Design Conditions: Towards a Portfolio of Organizational Capabilities, Interactive Practices and Individual Abilities, *Journal of Service Theory and Practice*, 27, 2, 384-407.

Krippendorff, K. (2006), *The Semantic Turn: A New Foundation for Design*, Taylor & Francis, Boca Raton.

Manzini, E. and F. Rizzo (2011), Small Projects/Large Changes: Participatory Design as an Open Participated Process, CoDesign, 7, 3-4, 199-215.

Walker, S. (2006), Sustainable by Design – Explorations in Theory and Practice, Earthscan, London.

GIULIA CALABRETTA
Delft University of Technology

GERDA GEMSER
RMIT University

INGO KARPEN
RMIT University

Conclusion

9.1

Strategic designers: Capital T-shaped professionals

The role of designers is changing. From a focus on specific innovation projects and design briefs to involvement in strategic decisions that frame these projects and briefs, designers are more and more shaping organizational strategy. While in the past designers would concentrate on enhancing desirability, the emerging strategic role of designers means that they have to balance desirability, feasibility and viability simultaneously. Designers need to expand their profiles and master the set of strategic practices proposed in this book so that all three design elements, in combination, lead to more successful outcomes.

Throughout this book we have proposed a series of practices that make strategic designers 'Capital T-shaped' professionals. These practices enable designers to understand and influence strategic decisions in terms of not only desirability, but also feasibility and viability. Figure 9.1 illustrates this. Strategic designers are those who have in-depth knowledge of and expertise in the field of desirability, that

is, in the fulfillment of (latent) human needs. As the vertical dimension in Figure 9.1 indicates, this ability lies at the core of the design profession.

In this book, we have shown how a focus on desirability can be leveraged for strategic purposes, for instance to define a vision (Chapter 1), as a focal point for the co-creation process (Chapter 2), or to create engaging customer stories (Chapter 5). In addition, some practices in this book enable designers to understand the feasibility and viability of innovation outcomes and strategies, so that they can effectively and efficiently collaborate with the other stakeholders involved in strategic decision-making. For example, Chapter 6 is focused on how to translate existing organizational resources and capabilities into feasible design outcomes; and Chapter 7 is focused on how to incorporate viability concerns into strategic design projects, thereby enhancing the degree to which strategic design outcomes are embraced by management.

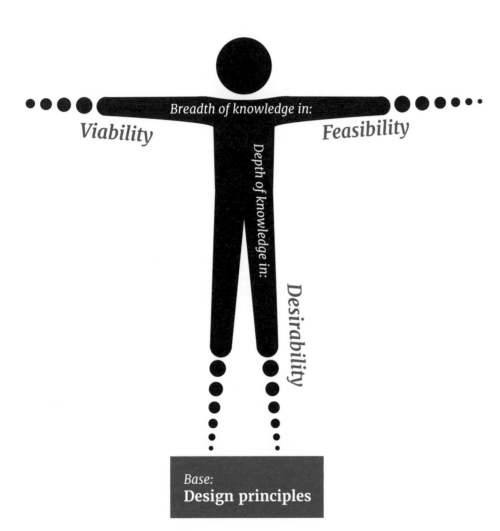

Figure 9.1: Capital T-shaped strategic designer

The dotted lines at the ends of the vertical and horizontal axes in figure 9.1 represent the idea that the strategic designer does not necessarily adhere to commonly accepted notions of desirability, viability and feasibility 'as they are', but tries to stretch these notions if he or she feels this is needed, to find and exploit exciting opportunities that will help make the current situation 'better'. This is how the chief design officer (CDO) role is currently perceived in many large organizations.

While the strategic designer aims to balance the demands of desirability, feasibility and viability, their own decisions and actions further rest on the six design principles outlined in Chapter 8 (see Figure 8.1: Make it about people; It's a team sport; Have a better-bias; Push for experimental uncovering; Enable a great story; See the bigger picture). These principles represent normative guidelines for viewing and making sense of the world of an organization, and how to behave in that world.

The eight practices presented in this book

9.2

Three-step approach for strategic design

teach designers to operate in ways that not only lead to successful outcomes, but using these working methods can also have lasting impact on the organization. The success of strategic design projects rests on designers' ability to generate acceptance and commitment for their strategic outcome *and* their designerly approach to it. Thus, in a strategic design task, the work designers do can dynamically affect the current offering, how the company operates, and even company vision and culture. Designers should take all this into account, and use the practices contained in this book to plan for the necessary structural and cultural changes to occur, and for the eventual implementation of the proposed changes. Designers can

approach the intervention and its implied transformations by following a three-step approach, as illustrated in figure 9.2.

The approach starts with a *preparation* stage where the intervention is planned and the company prepared. For this stage to be successful, designers must get to know and understand the company and its real challenges. Many of the practices illustrated in this book are relevant for this preparation stage, as they provide useful analytic tools that can be used to situate designers and their subsequent choices within the company ecosystem they are operating in: the simplifying practice (Chapter 3) helps designers to articulate the company vision and power structure, the structuring practice

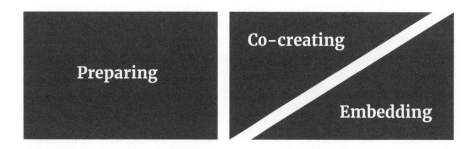

Figure 9.2: Model of the 3-Step approach to strategic design projects

(Chapter 4) helps them delineate the current innovation processes of a company, the translating practice (Chapter 5) helps designers to dissect and assess the organization's resources and capabilities, and the embedding practice (Chapter 7) starts by encouraging designers to understand the value drivers of a company in order to effectively operate within them.

Once the groundwork is laid, the design intervention occurs in the *co-creation* phase. Whatever strategic innovation assignment a designer is running – exploring business opportunities for a certain technology, creating an innovation vision, or designing a holistic brand experience – involving the stakeholders will be a fundamental part of it. If organizational stakeholders are invited to actively contribute to shaping the strategic design outcome, and to experience the design methods used themselves, designers can create acceptance and commitment.

Indeed, the topic of co-creation is covered in many of the chapters of this book (see Chapters 2, 4 and 8, for example). Design in general, and strategic design more specifically, is a 'team sport'. Ideally, designers should operate as part of a multidisciplinary team comprising specialists whose expertise lies in the realms of desirability, feasibility and viability. A perfect team for strategic purposes does not necessarily have to be large – a core team of five to six people is sufficient. Beyond this core, an extended team of subject matter specialists can operate as an 'advisory board' and consulted at various stages of the project lifecycle. Having an extended team, which might include technology experts or market analysts for example, is particularly useful when operating in larger organizations. Beyond this extended team lies the 'problem owner', together with other core decision-makers, if there are any. Problem owners are typically not part of the core team, particularly not in the case of large organizations, as the demands of their rank leave them little time for hands-on involvement with the core team. However, involving them and gaining their support for key decisions is paramount for the success of strategic innovation projects led by design professionals.

Given their expertise, strategic designers are often the best people to lead the team during the opportunity identification phase, although specialists should be given the latitude they need to perform viability and feasibility assessments. Viability and feasibility experts are the best people to lead the implementation phase, although designers still need to be able to safeguard desirability (see also Chapter 2).

Regardless of who takes the lead, co-creation should drive the project from its early stages until the completed implementation of the outcome. Maintaining this collaborative approach to the end can address one of the main challenges to designing for strategic impact – the limited involvement or even exclusion of designers during solution implementation. To secure sufficient influence during this phase, designers need to explain the benefit of their involvement from beginning to end right from the very start of the collaboration. The co-creation stage is accompanied/followed by an *embedding* stage, when designers (and the design team) evaluate their innovations, convince the stakeholders of the success of the outcomes, explain how to sustain the outcome and its success, and educate the company about how design practices, tools and methods can be main drivers for the organization's future innovation. This stage leads to permanent changes in internal processes and decisive shifts in the company mindset, both of which set the stage for dynamic future development.

Indeed, strategic designers are increasingly moving beyond project problem solving – many are helping organizations to build strategic design capacity (Chapter 8). Strategic designers thus morph into partners that help foster autonomous designerly thinking and acting. With this book we hope to have helped strategic designers feel ready to fulfill this role effectively.

Strategic design

Eight essential practices every
strategic designer must master

Giulia Calabretta,
Gerda Gemser &
Ingo Karpen